Corporates:

The Censored Stories

E.J. SABINO

Copyright © 2017 E.J. Sabino

All rights reserved.

ISBN-10: 1544983670
ISBN-13: 978-1544983677

ABOUT THE AUTHOR

E.J. Sabino is a Portuguese citizen of the world, that over the last two decades has lived in different European countries. Over that period of time, he had the opportunity to work in several major corporations, quite often occupying leadership positions. He has a large corporate experience both as a people leader and department manager. In his spare time he also covered major political events as a freelance journalist. He is an experienced traveler, an avid reader of books and a passionate believer in family values and professional integrity.

CONTENTS

		Page
1	The lady and her suitcase	9
2	Shampoo and credit cards	21
3	An expensive selfie	35
4	The KGB guardian angel	47
5	Paying to work	59
6	The accidental supervisor	71
7	Snipers at the office	83
8	Mentoring for idiots	95
9	The case of the sleepy engineer	107
10	The kinky director	119
11	Evaluation for dummies	131
12	A pocket full of money	143
13	A Christmas flood	155
14	The smartphone girl	167
15	Terrible bosses	179

DEDICATION

To all of those colleagues that have contributed, directly and indirectly, to the making of this manuscript.

To Ana for her brilliant illustrations, that portray with perfection the spirit of each one of the stories.

To Pedro for his detailed review of the texts and extremely useful insights.

To my wife Beata, without whom this book would never ever been published. Her constant support and creative ideas were fundamental to bring this project to life.

To my son Leo, as my source of inspiration.

Ultimately, to everyone that still believes that truth is more important than perception.

Thank you all from the bottom of my heart.

THE CENSORED STORIES

FOREWORD

E.J. SABINO

"You have not met the expectations!" - That sentence kept repeating itself, like a drumbeat in my head. As I walked, indifferent to the people passing by and unaware of the street names I was crossing, this was the only thought in my mind. I had no idea of what was the time of the day or what distance I had covered. I was walking for what it seemed an eternity and, although unaware of my surroundings, I was heading home. I knew I had a wife and a son waiting for me, after what should have been another day at the office. But it wasn't. I had been fired from the company I worked for. In fact, that was the second time that it happened in less than a year. I was 46 years old and unemployed.

I found all the support I needed in the affectionate embrace of my wife. I put things into perspective when I looked at the peaceful face of my son, sleeping in his bed. *"Have I met their expectations?"* was the question I made to myself. The love, care and attention that I got everyday from both of them told me that I was probably a good husband and a devoted father. But why, suddenly, after more than 20 years of working in corporations, I was no longer a good manager?

Sometimes it happens. You get too comfortable with your professional skills and your profile becomes outdated. Still, I didn't think that this was my case. I worked in highly technological companies, with all the latest trends and tools that a manager can learn and use. In any circumstance, it was not my lack of competency that seemed to be the problem. *"You didn't meet enough people in your 6 months in the company!"* - My last boss said. This, after I insisted in knowing the specific reasons why I was being dismissed. That sentence was the only argument she came up with. Apparently, I was not popular enough.

I grew up professionally believing that what makes a good employee is the ability to do the job that you are hired for. I never rushed in my career to try to get positions, just for the sake of their importance or the money they brought. I was always proud of being good at what I did and could not conceive a world where this would be secondary. In the past, a company would be happy if you did your job well. Not long ago, after my entire department got outsourced, I left the office under the applause of more than 50 people, praising me for the great manager I had been. It seems things changed in the meantime. So maybe yes, maybe I really became outdated and not the type of profile that companies are looking for nowadays.

The end result was that I started to have doubts about my professional capabilities. Perhaps this happened because those that fired me in a recent past were not able to say, with full clarity, why they were doing it. Even with a long experience behind your back, it's hard to listen that you are not a valid professional anymore. I could shout in the wind that I'm in my prime, that I'm a better manager now than I have ever been, that my skills are up-to-date and my leadership is my strongest quality. I could do that... but those would just be words that the wind would take. It seems that modern day corporates are sailing under a different type of breeze.

So here I am, a family man without a job. *"Should I try it again? Should I give it a shot in a different company?" "What options I have if the job that I'm experienced for is not there anymore?"* These and other million doubts overtook me in this delicate period of my life. Some people call it "soul searching", but it became apparent, as days passed, that it was time for a radical change. I began to ask myself a different type of questions. *"What did I really enjoy to do? What dreams did I keep in the back of my mind that remained unfulfilled? What type of job would make me happy in my professional life as I am in my personal life?"* It all came together when I realized that there was a common answer to all of those questions: Writing.

In my spare time, I've been writing a novel. For many years now, more than a hobby, it's something that I feel the need to do: tell stories. I'm not a fast writer and I need a peaceful environment to be able to write so, this means, that my novel progresses very slowly. Knowing this, my wife came up with an idea that later materialized into this book that you are about to read: *"Why don't you put your novel aside for a while and publish some of the stories from your professional life? I'm sure that there is a public out there eager to know what really happens in corporates."* - She said.

I gave the idea some thought and came to the conclusion that she was absolutely right. I've had my fair share of corporate jobs and I've witnessed and experienced a number of episodes that are worth being told. Not just because they provide a glimpse into the hidden side of what it means to work for such big companies, but also because I would like to confront the reader with their own individual aspirations and how much they match their current professional situation. The underlying question is simple: *"Are these jobs worth the effort?"*

These are stories about present day corporations. About how they appear to oversee the fact that human nature, with all its qualities and shortcomings, often overrules strict guidelines and office policies. As much as companies insist in selling their image of highly sophisticated and functional well-oiled-machines, the truth is that they are nothing more than the reflection of those that work for them. Occasionally, these stories also demonstrate that survival inside such organizations is more a question of whom do you know than a question of how well you work.

The people featured in this book are not isolated examples of exotic stories happening in offices around the globe. They symbolize some of the typical behaviors and common practices in many workplaces.

It's not their unique personalities and professional approach that it's relevant. It's the conclusion that they are not the exception to the rule but actually represent a bit of every office and every employee.

Finally, needless to say the names of the main characters are a product of my own imagination. The rest, the hard-core facts on which the stories are based upon, come from my own personal experience or the reports of trustworthy colleagues.

Quite often, in conversations with those that are closer to me, one of my best friends kept repeating the same sentence: *"If you ever tell these stories, nobody will believe you!"* Well, here I am doing precisely that and even if some of the episodes appear to be surreal, I can assure you that these are not even the most extravagant situations that I have experienced. Ultimately, I leave it up to you to believe in them or not.

I hope you enjoy reading this book. By doing so, you are already making my attempt to change my life worth it. Additionally, if it will help you chose an "happier" professional path for the future, then my accomplishment will be complete.

THE CENSORED STORIES

1 - THE LADY AND HER SUITCASE

THE CENSORED STORIES

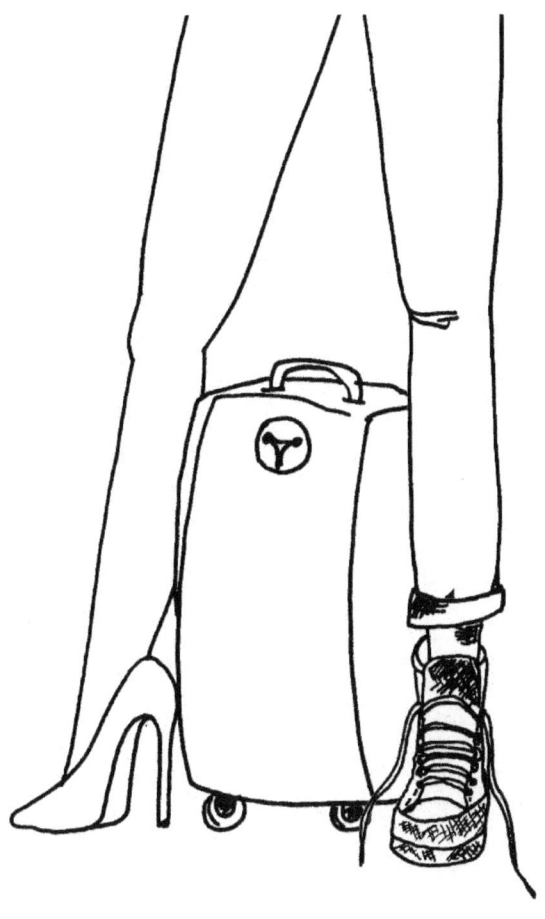

E.J. SABINO

Wheeling her travel suitcase, Veronica arrived to the office where she worked. A trivial scenario in the corporate world, where so many employees are constantly traveling, fulfilling their professional duties. However, this was not the case: Veronica didn't match with the stereotype of a company executive. Her attire was not one that you would normally associate with a professional trying to make a career in an international corporation. She was wearing a tank top that made visible a number of exotic tattoos in her arms and lower back. The jeans were casual and her blonde dyed hair had seen better days. In fact, it looked more that she was on her way to have coffee with friends instead of heading to the workplace.

She felt lucky to have landed a job in such a renowned enterprise. Yes, it was an entry level position, but it provided her with a steady income and the opportunity to (who knows) maybe even rise to higher assignments. Previously, she had been a shop attendant, but her knowledge of the English language was sufficient to convince the manager to offer her a chance as a customer service representative. Her colleagues, in the open-space office, never questioned the reason why she would bring a travel suitcase to the workplace. In any case, such detail would not be an attention grabber in an environment where one colleague would occasionally play the guitar during working hours and another would wear night slippers during his daily shifts.

The job was not precisely exciting: she spent her days entering data in a computer, checking some of the hundreds of emails that the team left unattended or taking the occasional call from a customer. The work demanded focus and detailed knowledge of the subject. However, the supervision was sluggish and the environment was more like a multinational Babylon of confused people trying to understand what their job was.

In the open office space, filled with endless rows of desks, she was seating in the middle of a row with three employees. On her left side, was a colleague that was a part-time cage fighter. Some days, he would show up with a bruised face or an injured limb. This happened so often that Veronica advised him that maybe it would be better if he would try a different sport. On her right side, a former plumber from New Zealand kept himself busy by surfing the web and choosing furniture for his newly acquired flat. Occasionally, he would leave the office in the middle of the day, because a new cabinet was going to be delivered and he needed to be at home to assemble the furniture. His productivity was so low that the supervisor hardly noticed when he was gone.

The office daily routine was so messed up, that they became indifferent to any changes or events that might affect them. A leadership change is usually big news in most organizations but that was not the case in Veronica's department. They had seen so many bosses come and go that the announcement of a new manager was hardly noticed. Veronica, however, was about to face one of the biggest frights of her life.

The recently appointed senior manager was on his way to make a first visit to his new operation. A meeting with employees was organized and everyone from Veronica's department was invited to attend. When the day came, a crowd of people gathered behind the reception area to know who was going to be their boss over the coming months (such was the "life expectancy" of the leaders in that department). The moment he entered the room she recognized him instantly. As he went through his short speech, she tried to hide behind the crowd, which was not easy, giving her tall complexion. He didn't seem to notice her presence or maybe pretended not to remember her.

Overwhelmed, Veronica returned to her desk and couldn't get herself to do some work for the rest of the afternoon. The reason for her distress was simple: she had another profession besides being a customer service clerk for eight hours a day. Her other activity didn't pay taxes and required little technical skills. On a glamorous website, she offered her company to highly respectable and wealthy gentlemen. Those seeking her attention would pay a fee and all the associated expenses, to enjoy a few hours of her bubbly character and exquisite beauty. Veronica was an escort.

Shockingly, the truth was that the newly appointed senior manager had been one of her former customers. On a not so distant past, she had been required to travel to the so-called glamorous city of London. In the company of another lady, she had been "invited" to fulfill the lustful wishes of a certain gentleman. The visit was a feast of champagne and gourmet meals that ended up with an infamous threesome. Their host had a vivid fantasy and he had, at last, achieved one of his life goals: to share a bed with two beautiful ladies. This same person was now the leader of her organization.

That was, in fact, the reason why Veronica carried a suitcase to the office: while she was handling requests and customers orders, some of them of substantial value, she would keep a vigilant eye on her mobile phone. At any moment, a call from her other "*employer*" would require her immediate availability. The rest was easy: her supervisor became used to her sudden requests to be excused from work. Veronica told him that her chronicle back pain required regular doctor visits. So, she would just complain about an acute surge of the pain and, with the supervisor's agreement, leave the office in a rush, wheeling her suitcase along the way. In a matter of hours, Veronica would be flying to meet her next customer.

She would return a few days later, justifying herself for any inconvenience caused. A paper from the family doctor, that happened to be a regular customer of her other *"professional skills"*, would appease the supervisor and guarantee the legality of her non-attendance. The daily routine would settle again, with her mailbox bursting at the seams, her colleagues in a haze of blissful daydreaming and customers unaware that their issues were being handled by such a crowd of people.

The rigid rules of the corporation, its code of conduct, the company culture and values, all of that looked meaningless in the day-to-day life of that customer support operation. It was a survival game and each individual tried to do what they thought would best serve their interests. Most of them had other jobs to supplement their monthly income. Veronica's expensive taste for handbags and designer shoes couldn't be supported by the salary paid by the company. She felt that her escort services were nothing more than a legitimate way of providing her a better life. She had no regrets.

Fortunately - for Veronica - the new manager was not based in the same office. He might visit regularly but he would still be working from a different branch, situated in another country. Her initial panic faded away as she realized that, even if he would recognize her, the manager would have no personal interest in denouncing her to HR.

She was right. He had known who she was from the first time he had laid his eyes on her. How could he forget a lady that provided him with such an unforgettable experience in life? He waited to see what would be her reaction but, as weeks passed and he heard nothing from her, his concerns also disappeared. He knew that if anything came out it would be a huge scandal and dismissal was certain. In the end, he would have more to lose than she would.

Months went by and everything went back to normal. However, Veronica grew uncomfortable with her situation. She didn't appreciate that both her jobs had mixed together. She couldn't come to terms that she was frequently sharing the office with someone that had been a client in her other *"secret world"*. She avoided his looks when he was around but that didn't make her forget that, after all, she had slept with the big boss. Also, her supervisor became increasingly annoyed with her excuses for the unexpected absences. He now kept a close eye on her productivity and she was far from happy about it. Fed up, Veronica decided to leave the company.

She resigned a couple of months later, leaving the disorderly world of that customer support operation. She never knew if the manager had recognized her or not. If he did, she thought, he had done a great job disguising it. They had briefly been together in meeting rooms (never on a one to one basis) and he gave no sign of remembering her or what they had done together. She soon found a similar role in another company, with an even slightly better salary. As for the manager, he only lasted a couple of months more. The prophecy of short-lived leaderships in that department had once again been fulfilled. He moved on with his career.

Sometime later, Veronica's alternative duties came to

the knowledge of local HR. They were outraged that such a character had been able to find a job in their company. As a result, the hiring process was updated, with a more rigorous screening of the candidate's background.

While her previous company got more stringent on recruitment, other firms seemed to take a less rigid approach. Veronica still managed to work in a number of other corporations before "retiring" from all her professional duties, when she finally met a respectable wealthy American gentleman that made all her dreams come true.

2 - SHAMPOO AND CREDIT CARDS

THE CENSORED STORIES

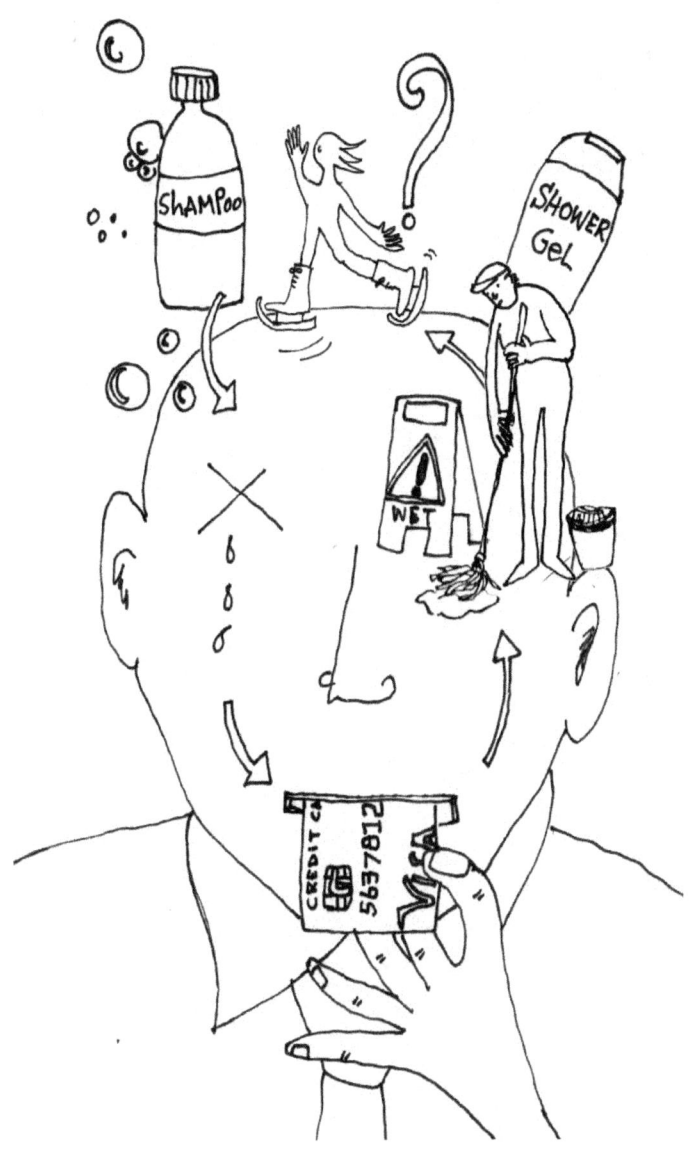

E.J. SABINO

It was just another day at the office. That early morning, the manager struggled to keep his eyes open, while going through a packed mailbox. *"I'm getting so many spam emails these days"* – he thought, while endlessly scrolling the screen. One of the emails came from a senior vice-president and it had a picture attached: the CEO of the company showing up, once more, in the front cover of an international magazine. The caption, placed just below the big boss smiling face, stated *"CEO of the year"*. In smaller letters, the cover also mentioned: *"The CEO who managed to get his company through the crisis without firing anyone."* *"That's interesting"* - the manager thought - *"Didn't we just outsource an entire department and 300 hundred people lost their job? Well, maybe the journalist skipped that part"*. He deleted the email and proceeded to the next one.

The manager worked for a multi-billion dollar company, with thousands of employees and offices around the globe. Its smiling CEO was a man of a certain reputation, an influential figure that had regular meetings with the highest levels of power, including the president of the United States of America. Who wouldn't be proud to be working for such a company and such an inspiring leader? Well, on that day the emails kept coming, one after the other, and our manager didn't feel exactly inspired. His only wish was to be somewhere else instead of that office.

In the meantime, another email caught his attention. This one was coming from the highest levels of the Human Resources department and the topic was the misuse, by employees, of the corporation's credit cards. In the past, everyone joining the company was entitled to receive a credit card, regardless of the position they were to occupy. That policy had been abandoned recently as it was often subject to abuse. One of the most significant episodes, that lead to the policy change, was when a newly recruited sales guy used all the credit from his card and disappeared the next day, never to be found again. Now, only those in leadership positions were allowed to keep their cards. Nonetheless, it appeared that this restriction had not been enough to stop the abuses.

The email stated that *"accounting reports continued to display a significant number of transactions, made with the corporate credit cards that were not within the scope of business activities"*. Basically, people were using the company's money like if it was their own.

Several examples were provided of those irregular charges such as:

- Someone had bought flower bouquets for a

series of romantic "*rendez vous*!";
- The company had paid a fabulous wedding dress for the daughter of one of the employee's;
- Private cars had been repaired with the use of the corporation card;
- House mortgage payments were done using the "free credit";
- The company even "involuntarily sponsored" extravagant purchases such as two hundred liters of screen-washing fluid.

Those misusing the card were urged to stop such behaviors or the company would have to take additional measures to prevent further wrongdoing. That was another way to say that they would be fired.

The manager tried to remember the last time he had used his company card but it had been such a long time ago that he couldn't even recall for what purpose he had done it. Maybe a business trip or something of the kind. Anyway, he got himself a cup of tea and checked his watch, as the first meeting of the day was about to start. His thoughts were left lingering on that email about credit cards misuse as it reminded him of a story that had recently come to his knowledge. Not long ago, his boss (director, as well as responsible for the entire office) approached him in search of advice. The manager felt honored by such a display of trust but his mood quickly changed when he heard the whole story.

The director had a significant number of employees reporting to him, including two people responsible for quality and training. Sometime ago, both of them were sent to a very important meeting taking place in the company's headquarters in the US. The whole event lasted a full week, but after that, both the Quality lady and the Training gentleman, decided to take a week off and explore the country. It was the first time that both of them were traveling to American lands and they wanted to enjoy the experience.

After those two weeks they returned to the office and submitted the expenses made during their trip. The only step left was to wait for the director's approval and the process would be completed. However, when their boss verified the amount and the nature of the expenses they made, he almost had a heart attack. The credit cards had been used to pay a variety of expenses that had nothing to do with the business trip or with the duties related to the event that they attended.

The list was quite impressive:

- While they had been on vacation, they rented a car to better explore the endless highways of the country ;
- Naturally, they visited the glamorous cities of Las Vegas and Los Angeles and hotel bills were paid by the company;
- No trip is perfect without extensive shopping expeditions to clothes and shoe shops, especially when they are bought using "foreign" credit;
- To keep their spirits in the best mood

possible, they also visited fancy restaurants, where delicious meals were served;
- Finally, an invoice from a jewelry shop was the last classy touch of a memorable week, "sponsored" by the corporation card.

The credit limit of one of the cards had been reached and the other one was very close to it. The conclusion was obvious: both cards had been used to pay not only for the business trip, but also for the employee's vacation. The amounts were unjustifiable and there were no arguments that could support the approval of those expenses.

The director decided to have a conversation with both of them. First he met the quality specialist. The lady recognized immediately that she had used the card for all of her expenses, including those of a private nature. She apologized profusely, cried a little bit and confessed that she had lost control and had even spent all of her personal money as well. She tried to justify herself by saying that the *"great bargains that she found in American shops were irresistible!"*. When the director insisted that he could not approve such expenses, she begged him to do so. She promised to reimburse the company for all the amounts related to her private amusement and shopping.

The trainer said more or less the same, with the exception that he had not reached the credit limit on the card, so his situation was a little bit better than his colleague's. He said he had tried to restrain himself from using the card, but his traveling partner was so enthusiastic about knowing new things and visiting new places, that he ended up going along with it. He also asked for his expenses to be approved and swore that he would return back every penny.

To make matters worse, the director was now getting feedback from the other attendees of the US event and the news were far from positive. People were complaining that his employees had spent most of the time giggling, playing around or surfing their social network pages during the meetings. The organizer was requesting an explanation for such an unprofessional behavior. The boss had to write a long email asking for forgiveness and promising *"a swift action to prevent any further wrongdoing from his direct reports"*.

So those were the circumstances that had led the director to ask for advice. The manager heard the story and promptly asked:

- *So, what are you going to do?*

The boss shook his head and, with a serious expression, replied:

"I don't know. On one side, they are both good employees and they fulfill their duties. On the other side, their behavior was unacceptable and they have broken the company's policies."

The manager shrugged and said:

"Well, we are all suppose to be good employees and fulfil our duties. That's what we are paid for. However, if you break the

rules, you have to suffer the consequences. If you approve those expenses, you are opening the door to further misuse of company credit cards."

He felt that this was not the answer that his boss wanted to listen:

"Look, I get what you are saying", the director replied, *"but they are both knowledgeable and difficult to replace. You know them, they are nice people as well. I don't think I should fire them for what they did."*

The manager stretched himself in the office chair. He looked straight in the eyes of his boss:
"I see your point and understand that it's a tough decision to make, but it can't be based on personal likes or dislikes. Even if you don't fire them, you have to make sure this doesn't happen again. Take the cards from them, give them some warnings or something but don't just approve their expenses or you will be also breaching the company's policies."

The boss didn't like this last remark and his expression became stern. Probably he thought that he shouldn't be listening such preaching from someone who was reporting directly to him. He thanked the manager for the advice and left his office shortly after. They never spoke again about the subject, but the manager was made aware of what happened afterwards: the expense reports were approved and both employees were allowed to repay the amounts over the following months. They kept their company cards and were not the subject of any disciplinary actions.

That story stayed in the manager thoughts throughout the day. It reminded him of one of the unwritten rules of office work: you can bend company policies to the same extent that your boss likes you... or not!

The end of the day came up, with an unplanned meeting between the manager and one of his employees. She was a very bubbly lady with a complete lack of sense of what means to be "politically correct".

She lost no time:

"I've requested this meeting just to make a quick question, if you don't mind."

"Sure, go ahead", replied the manager, hardly able to hide his tired expression.

"It's a topic that we have been discussing with the team for a while without reaching any conclusion so... I decided to ask you. Since you are bald, do you still use shampoo when taking a bath or just shower gel?"

The manager burst into laughter. He had spent the whole day in endless meetings and (mostly) meaningless email exchanges. He had left his mind wonder about credit cards and company policies. And now, there he was, challenged to answer a question that could probably decide the future of mankind. He caressed his bald head for a few moments, while trying to regain his composure. He was happy that someone had managed to put things into perspective.

"Yes, I can confirm that I still use shampoo, if that's what you need to know", he replied with a smile on his face.

The lady left the office proud of her achievement. She had solved the riddle. What she didn't know was that she also had made the manager´s day.

3 - AN EXPENSIVE SELFIE

Anita had none of the skills required for the job but she decided to apply anyway. Her native language wasn't English but she knew it quite well and, hopefully, this would give her a decisive advantage during the recruitment process. On top of that, Anita thought that her pleasant looks would also work in her favor, as she knew how to impress the hiring managers. After just two interviews, Anita got the job and she was thrilled about it. Yes, her boss looked a little bit nerdy and old fashioned, but she was certain that her charm would conquer him quickly.

Her work was far from being complex but, nevertheless, it required accuracy and focus. She found it boring and uninteresting. In any case, the position gave her a relatively good salary and, for a provincial girl that had recently moved to the country´s capital, that income kept her bills paid. Besides that, her duties required a permanent contact with other departments and soon she started to entertain hopes of getting herself a different role. One that would be better off financially and more prestigious.

She managed to pass the three months long probation period. However, conquering the sympathy of her old-fashioned boss revealed itself a much harder task than she had anticipated. He was quite a peculiar figure, completely different from all the other managers, with an extreme devotion to his work. Some said that he was just a workaholic, spending sixteen hours a day in the office. For Anita, though, it wasn't the long hours at work that made him an odd person. She was mostly shocked by his fashion sense or, let's say, the lack of it. It was like if his wardrobe had been bought in the eighties and had never been renewed. Another strange thing about him was that his lunch was a ham and cheese sandwich... every single day. *"What a crackpot!"* she would think, especially on the occasions he would wear a tie featuring a mouse eating cheese.

Months passed and the team's workload kept increasing. It was a small group of only four people, but the manager always said yes to every department that dumped a task on them. He was this type of personality that is incapable of saying no to senior leaders and, as a result, he would end up overloading his own team. Although he was a pretty much hands-on type of manager, working even during weekends, it came to a point that it was just too much work to be handled by such a small team. Anita and her colleagues protested but he would have none of it. Instead, he decided to demand even more commitment from them, ignoring the complains.

Ultimately though, he was allowed to hire a fifth employee. Everybody in the team welcomed the new joiner and they were even happier when he completed his training successfully. The impact he made was immediately felt by everyone, since slowly, but surely, their workload got under control. The manager was also satisfied, as the results improved, although he still worked long hours everyday. Nevertheless, he now had time to deal with a different type of issues. He wasn't too pleased how the team had behaved during the most stressful periods and he decided to do something about it. The main target was Anita and she knew exactly why.

Punctuality had never been one of her qualities. She always struggled to arrive on time to her personal engagements and on her professional life she was no different. The disapproving looks she got from her boss, every time she was the last one to arrive to the office, made her wonder how long she would be able to keep herself out of trouble. She also got easily distracted during the working hours and this resulted in regular mistakes from her side. Sooner than later, Anita knew that her boss would make her accountable for her shortcomings. It was just a matter of time.

It turned out that she was right. Her manager called her to a meeting and, sure enough, made her aware of his dissatisfaction with some aspects of her performance. Accuracy in following the processes and timekeeping were not up to the expectations and he came up with a plan to tackle those flaws. First, she would have to stay longer every time that she would arrive late to the office in order to compensate the company for her lateness. Second, her work was going to be closely monitored and, if any more mistakes would be found, she would have to go through a formal performance improvement program.

"*What a nuisance!*" Anita thought. At this point she had been with the company for over a year and, as a result of that meeting, her determination to find another position increased. She was certain that her charms would catch the attention of another manager and she would be able to move forward quite quickly. Her jealous female colleagues whispered that she looked "*too flirty and easy*" but she would dismiss all the gossip around her. "*This is war and I intend to use all weapons at my disposal!*" Anita mumbled, while running to the office, trying not to be late once again.

Her chances were slim but the Gods of the corporate Olympus came to the rescue. A temporary ban on external hiring was enforced in all departments and open positions could only be fulfilled by internal candidates. This was the breakthrough that Anita was waiting for. She was now sure that, soon enough, she would get another job in the company. Her expectations were not defrauded and, quicker than a blink of an eye, she was accepted for another position - a lateral move but in a more prestigious role. As an extra bonus, she got rid of the annoying boss and was now able to start afresh.

The new job, as a customer support back-office

agent, was a lot easier than her previous one. The supervisor had a more relaxed approach and the pace of work was slower. She adapted well to these new circumstances and, for a while, Anita enjoyed a peaceful time in corporate life. She was still regularly getting late to work and made the odd mistake, but that didn't seem to affect her job stability. The truth, however, was that her manager wasn't too happy with her performance but, since he couldn't hire anyone else, he chose the lesser of two evils: instead of being understaffed he would rather keep her, even if she was one of the weakest members of the team.

A year passed and Anita not only got extremely bored with her role but also started to entertain the idea that it was, once more, time to move her career forward. Again, the Gods of the corporate Olympus were favorable to her aspirations. One manager was particularly fascinated by Anita's charms. It happens that he also had an open position in his team so, naturally, she was accepted as a valid candidate. After one single interview, where her lack of experience for the role was not considered an obstacle, Anita finally managed to rise in the career ladder: she became an internal auditor, having spent less than 3 years in the company. Her skills were far from being the ones that the job demanded but her enthusiastic boss wasn't too concerned about it and, therefore, so wasn't she. All stars seemed to be aligned and Anita's brilliant future was guaranteed.

Once again, she adapted to her new environment with the carelessly of someone that was always ready for novelty and change. Feeling protected by her manager, she took her time to learn the skills of the trade and embody the respectful (and respected) duty of an auditor. She was happy and her new colleagues appeared to be pleased as well. Anita felt invincible.

Unfortunately, however, her wonderful career was bound to be shattered by an unforeseen mistake. Always eager to celebrate her success and a fan of social media networks, she picked up her smartphone and took a selfie at work. Nothing odd, she had done this plenty of times before and since she was feeling particularly glamorous, a beautiful photo of herself would only make the day brighter. Sadly enough, that innocent selfie had something more to it than Anita's pretty face. She had taken the photo having one of the company's boards as a background. Behind her, quite visible in the board, a few documents were posted with confidential information. She barely noticed it while sharing her glorious picture in one of the most popular social media websites.

In her path through the company's career ladder, Anita had been followed by a legion of critics and gossipers, most of them former team colleagues. They were unhappy about the way how she had risen in the hierarchy - without proven skills - and how she always seemed to be able to escape from the tight spots where she got herself into. One of her rivals was thrilled to see the careless photo that she had posted and quickly denounced it to senior leadership. The selfie was analyzed and the evidence was overwhelming: it was fairly easy to read the internal policies on the background of the picture. Anita's manager was instructed to act harshly.

The next day he called her to a meeting, which she attended with a big smile on her face. She liked the meetings with her new boss, as he was always very kind and had a great sense of humor. However, he looked too serious this time. Had she done something wrong?

"I'm afraid this meeting is not for the best reasons", said the manager. *"We have something serious to discuss."*

"What is it?" asked Anita, hardly disguising the anxiety that was taking over her.

"Well... it seems that you took a photo of yourself at work yesterday and, by posting it in social media, you have made public some confidential information about the company."

Anita immediately realized that the conversation was about the previous day selfie. She had paid no attention to what was written behind her and had no idea that it was important.

"Oh, I see, it's about the selfie I took yesterday", she said, *"I'm sorry about that, I had no idea that there was some important stuff behind me. I will delete it, if that's what you want."*

"I wish it was as simple as that", he replied with a sorrow tone on his voice, *"but unfortunately it's more complicated. Disclosure of confidential information is a serious breach of company policy. I'm afraid I will have to dismiss you!"* concluded the manager, with a sigh.

At first, Anita was genuinely shocked. However, she recovered quickly and used all the tricks in the book to have the manager's decision reversed. She even shed a tear or two but nothing worked. As much as he would have liked to continue to develop their professional relationship, he could not ignore the company's strict rules. He concluded the meeting offering a letter of recommendation, so she would be able to continue her career elsewhere. Seeing that all her efforts were in vain, she dismissed the offer and headed to HR, where the documents confirming her departure were already waiting.

A few days later, while searching for a new job, Anita reflected for a moment on the whole incident. She felt that she had paid the ultimate price for a simple photo and her rising career was now destroyed. Next time, she promised to herself, she would be much more careful. The important thing was that now her confidence was restored and she was certain that another great job was waiting for her. Her CV was full of rich experiences from the last 3 years, a far cry from the one that had landed her the first role in a corporate. She was determined to aim higher than ever before.

4 - THE KGB GUARDIAN ANGEL

"*How* did he manage to get a job here?" the team wondered.

"*How come did he get such an influential position as director for export compliance?*" commented his co-workers during coffee breaks.

His name was Victor and he was the main topic in office conversations. He had a very peculiar manner and a very enigmatic behavior. It was not only the fact that he would be often closed in his office, in conference calls that would last for hours. "*Probably he is a very busy person!*" they tried to guess. Above all, it was the decoration he chose for his office that grabbed the attention of everyone passing by. The walls were covered with diplomas and certificates written in Cyrillic alphabet. However, as far as his colleagues knew, Victor was not Russian.

What made it more awkward was that Victor was an employee of a big American corporation, although his particular office was located in Europe. He was also dealing with very sensitive information, which was usually only available to a very restricted number of employees. Nothing of that seemed to concern the company's leadership and Victor just carried on with his job, displaying a very unique attitude. Slowly, but surely, he became one of the most popular characters of office folklore.

Visually, he could hardly go unnoticed. He had a very peculiar taste in shirts, more specifically splashy Hawaiian fabrics. His insistence in wearing those colorful shirts, even in the peak of Winter, was something hardly ignored by those who happen to cross him in office corridors. His trademark fashion statement was reinforced by what became a regular vision to those arriving to work every morning! Outside, seating in a bench close to the building entrance, Victor would be seen holding documents in one hand and a Cuban cigar in the other. In freezing winter mornings, his short sleeved-shirt offered a colorful contrast to the snow that covered the ground.

Besides his very unique dress code, Victor became also known for his poor sense of humor. On a monthly basis, as part of his duties, he would provide export compliance training. Those thirty minute sessions were filled with boring guidelines and customs regulations that were hardly an interesting topic to present. Aware of that, Victor tried to make some jokes along the way, attempting to lighten up the subject and stimulate the audience. The problem was that his talent to be funny was non-existent and the best he could get from the attendees was a baffled expression. To make matters worse, the highlight of his comic performance were comments such as:

"It seems you didn't find it funny. Well, at least my wife laughs at my stupid jokes! Maybe because she is stupid herself!" he would say, giggling along the way.

During those training sessions, expressions of old or new employees went very quickly from baffled to utter shock.

Everyone knew by now that being politically correct was not one of Victor's biggest strengths. His colleague's opinion of him balanced between perplexity and amusement. They found him funny because he was not funny at all. On the other hand, they would be often amazed with some of his statements. Jokingly, once he even confessed that in the past, he had worked for the KGB. Strange enough, occasionally, he would be seen talking Russian on his mobile phone and he would bring strange people to his office, that nobody knew who they were. *"Could it be that he was still a spy?"* people often wondered.

Leadership, however, seemed to be happy with him. The only incident came when, after less than a year on the job, he demanded a significant pay rise or he *"would leave the company immediately"*. His superiors were a bit surprised by this sudden threat but promised to take a look at it during the yearly performance review.

In the meantime, slowly but surely, another important feature of Victor's character became known: he liked to bring a number of *protégés* under his wing and propel their careers forward. Although Victor was far from being a womanizer, he was keen to champion the cause of a restricted number of ladies. His choices seemed to be random, except for one of the call center workers that had been a university colleague in the past. She was a bit older than him and a remarkable lady in the contact center platform. She was also like fish out of water in her current role: incapable of interacting with her much younger colleagues and unable to understand the basic principles of her job. Victor appeared as an unexpected guardian angel and she took every opportunity to spend time chatting with him in his office.

Nonetheless, even with all his goodwill, Victor soon realized that his former university colleague was just too incompetent to be sponsored for a career move. The last drop of his patience was exhausted when she visited him in the office and, with an expression of outrage, said that a customer had tried to call her that morning. Victor couldn't understand:

"But... isn't that what you are suppose to do on that job?" he asked.

"The others can take calls, I'm too experienced to do such tasks!" was her outraged reply.

With a sigh, Victor realized that she was good for a coffee chat but, as a professional, she was useless.

Besides his interest in the customer service

department, he also invested his time in helping the office coordinators. That was the fancy title that the company had for a receptionist job. He quickly became a sort of patron to all of the office ladies who were in that role and, using his influence, he promoted their skills with managers that had open positions. On this mission he obtained several successes, the biggest of them all was to turn a few ladies into office managers, less than 6 months after they joined the company. With one of his favorite *receptionists*, he took things even further and hired her as a direct report, to support him on his export compliance duties.

His expertise in finding talent expanded to other senior positions as well. In one occasion, he had a decisive role in the recruitment of one of the managers. The job was quite a challenging one as it involved a large team that was continuously growing. Victor ignored the poor curriculum and lack of experience of one of the candidates and campaigned heavily for her selection. His gut feeling told him she was a good fit for the role and his persistence did the rest. He rallied support from other leaders and she got the job.

Victor was far from guessing that this recruitment process would be the beginning of his own downfall. Although he always behaved in a very professional manner, without the slightest hint that he was taking advantage of the ladies, his "sponsorship programs" were only tolerated as far as his *protégés* would prove to be competent. The new manager, whom he had been so eager to promote, revealed herself as a complete disaster.

Her inability to manage and become a real leader of her organization was beyond any possible solution. As months progressed, the results got worse and the department was left in complete disarray. Victor visited her office frequently but she couldn't get a grip on things and his advises produced no effect at all on her performance. He thought several times about replacing the disastrous manager. However, he had invested so much in making her join the company that he was left with no other option than making sure that she was successful or his reputation would be in tatters.

Ultimately, he had to surrender to the evidence. After another damaging report on the progress of her department, Victor went to her office, determined to give the lady manager an ultimatum. As soon as he opened the door, his jaw dropped: she was at her desk in the company of one of her team members. In her hand she had a joystick and both seemed to be heavily absorbed in playing a flight simulator game. Seeing Victor, she reacted candidly:

"Give it a try, Victor. It's a really funny game to play!" she said, without any sign of embarrassment.

From that episode on-wards, Victor stopped any contact with the lady, until she was eventually fired a few months later. His previous successes in promoting other people's careers were undoubtedly obscured by that spectacular failure. His reaction was not the best either: he became bitter and disappointed, isolating himself from the rest of his colleagues. At the same time, his boss received an increasing amount of complaints about Victor´s favoritism towards certain employees and his unprofessional remarks during training sessions. Victor realized that, as time passed, his colleagues came to resent his guardian angel activities. He felt like a soldier in enemy territory.

The salary increase that he requested never materialized. Although his job seemed secure, Victor was not so keen in pursuing a career in a company were his merits as a talent promoter and coaching guru were not properly recognized. In a very cold February morning as usual, he was seating outside, apparently indifferent to the freezing temperatures. As he watched people pass by, wrapped in their coats, with red cheeks and dripping noses, he made the decision to leave the company. He was certain that he was made for much higher flights than that office could offer. He resigned that same day.

He was right. A few years later he became the CEO of a big company, enjoying all the privileges and perks that such position has to offer. Indeed, it was not a global corporation, but it was big enough to make him feel at the top of the world. Interestingly enough, some of his *protégés* also did well in their careers, including his former university colleague. She managed to secure a position in the credit department. However, to this day, similar to what happened in her previous role, she has no clue of what her job is about.

5 - PAYING TO WORK

THE CENSORED STORIES

Jack could hardly believe what he was experiencing. As much as he would try to see the issue from different angles, the reality was that he was being asked to pay for working. Not in the literal term of having to bring money so he could seat in the office, but if the company had required cash in advance from him, what else could that be called? He decided to turn off his computer and go home. During the 40 minutes long commute he would have more than enough time to think about his professional dilemma.

He had been in the company for about 3 months. His first impressions were not exactly positive. The office seemed to be riddled with petty politics, back-stabbing and "management upon whim" behaviors. Still, Jack was trying to settle in, making an effort to learn the job and avoid any incidents that could compromise his status during the six-month long probation period. Training had been poor and insufficient. He had spent one week in a classroom, where he watched presentation after presentation with generic information about the company. Then, he was left alone to carry on with his job. Under these circumstances, he relied heavily on his professional experience to be able to successfully secure his position.

After one of the many meetings he had with his boss, Jack was informed that he would be required to make some business trips. During the recruitment process he was made aware that his position as Operations Manager would involve something like 20% of his time spent in traveling, so the news came as no surprise. Certainly he was not expecting to have to travel to three different countries in consecutive weeks, but he took it as an opportunity to get to know people from other offices and get a better feeling how the company really worked.

Trip arrangements were to be discussed over the following days but that was a task that Jack was not concerned about. He had no company credit card, which was something that he was used to from his previous jobs. However, since now he worked for a travel company, he was certain that booking flights and hotels would be an easy thing to do. He was asked to contact one of the administrative assistants to handle all preparations.

That's when things started to look weird. When discussing the trip details with her he was asked if he would be providing his personal credit card info, or, alternatively, if his boss would pay directly. Jack only had a debit card, mainly because the expenses related to getting a credit card in that country were not exactly affordable. Trying to hide his surprise, he asked: *"Why would you need my credit card details? Don't you just have a company account and use it to book flights and hotels?"* The answer he heard was that there was no such thing as a company account, and that everyone traveling had to pay all expenses from their own pockets and then submit them for reimbursement. As an alternative, the boss personal card could be used to pay some of the expenses, but her authorization was required for that to happen. Jack was astonished.

Yes, he heard about other companies where employees had to pay part of their traveling expenses in advance, but he never heard of a case where they had to pay for everything. Jack was also aware that, in some countries, where a big part of the population has credit cards, that was a common corporate practice. His case was different. He was living in a nation where the use of credit cards was not widespread and they were still seen as a luxury by most of the population. Ultimately, the biggest issue was that he was being asked to commit part of his monthly salary to pay for some of his business duties. Reimbursements would usually take up to ten business days, meaning he could potentially be waiting half a month for his money to be returned. He had a wife and a son to support, so that scenario was not something he could accept.

In the next meeting with his boss, Jack explained that he was very surprised with the company's business travel policy. He also told her that this kind of information was something he should have been made aware of during the recruitment process. The director dismissed his concerns, confirming she would pay for flights and hotels with her own credit card, so he would only have small expenses to worry about. However, she also shared with him one additional company policy: when traveling with a group of people, the most senior person was responsible for paying all of the expenses. That left Jack even more worried: in one of the upcoming trips he would be traveling together with three of his direct reports. After the meeting, he felt confused and in disbelief. The reality was that his hardly won money was (partially) at the disposal of the corporate he worked for.

Weeks passed and Jack decided not to worry too much about the trips and the company policies. He would test things himself and see if it was as bad as it looked. In the meantime, he questioned some of his colleagues about the travel policy and found out that, in one way or another, they were all against it. However, the common thought was that nothing could be done to change it.

One of the stories that Jack heard was particularly alarming: in the past, one of the supervisors had been asked, at short notice, to join a training in the company's headquarters in the US. It was a two-week long event and since he had to pay for all of the trip's expenses, he was forced to ask for a loan to a bank. *"How come people get to the point of compromising their personal finances just to be able do something for the company?"* Jack asked, with an expression of amazement.

The trips finally happened, in consecutive weeks. There was only time to get home, unpack, repack and leave again. For almost a full month, Jack and some of his colleagues lived in a frantic rhythm of flights, hotels, meetings, workshops and endless introductions followed by team building events. His personal debit card was used over and over again, mostly to pay meals and taxi rides. Twice however, he was caught completely by surprise when he found out that the hotel had not been paid in advance, as it had been promised. In one of these occasions, he had no other option but to pay for his stay as well as the hotel bill of three of his colleagues. His bank account got depleted very fast.

At the end of those three weeks, it was time to assess the damage that his personal finances had suffered. He had received his monthly salary a few days before his business trips had started. After one week, he had already spent half of it. By the end of all his business travels, he had spent his full salary. He now had to go to an online tool, submit all the receipts and, after an approval from his boss, the period of ten days would begin and he would eventually get his money back. Jack was in a state of despair. He had now to survive the rest of the month until the next salary would be paid.

When he got home, he wasn't sure how to explain to his wife that they would have to use some of their economies until he would get his money back. It all seemed surreal. His wife just couldn't understand how a multi-million dollar company would ask this from its employees: *"Why nobody complains? Why they don't do something to change it?"* she asked, with a tone of incredulity in her voice. Jack had made those same questions himself and all he got were vague answers.

In the meantime, they were left with no other option but to go to their bank and withdraw some money from their savings account.

More bad news followed: Jack was now certain that he wouldn't get all of his money back. The reason for this was related to exchange rates. He had been exposed to different currencies during those trips. His bank charged him fees and used inflated exchange rates, every time he made a payment abroad. These fees and taxes were not reflected in any of the receipts that he would claim for reimbursement. Therefore, he was literally losing money by traveling on corporate duty. *"I never thought I would have to pay to work!"* repeated Jack to his wife, in one the recurrent conversations they had about the topic.

Counting every penny, Jack's family survived until, eventually, his money was reimbursed. Determined to never experience such difficulties again, Jack made a decision: he wrote an email to his boss saying he could not comply with the company's business travel policy. He also stated that he would only make another trip if all the expenses would be paid in advance. His boss never replied to the email and on face to face conversations dismissed the subject as of minor importance. Nonetheless, a promise was made to seek a solution for his particular case.

In the meantime, as weeks passed, Jack was made aware of another of the company's bizarre policies: supervisors had a monthly budget for team building events and the money *had* to be spent. The company had an agreement with some venues where teams could enjoy food and drinks, with the cost being invoiced directly to the corporate. However, those were just a few. This meant that, quite often, supervisors had to pay the whole thing out of their own pockets. The monthly budget for team building events was equivalent to at least half of their salaries. To keep the team members happy, the company "asked" the supervisors to pay for it, meaning they had to "reserve" half of their wage to follow company rules. Jack had no idea how his colleagues managed to live for the rest of the month.

These strange procedures made the new Operations Manager wonder if that was the right place for him to work. He had thought about quitting several times but, since he had a family to support and no other job in sight, he had made up his mind to stay and try changing things from the inside. He thought his experience could help improve things and even change some of those policies. He also hoped that people would be more vocal in complaining about those rules that interfered with their personal lives.

He never came to put those plans in practice. After six months, in the last hour of his probation period, Jack was fired by his boss. She claimed that he had not met the expectations the company had when he was hired. That was his last surprise in that office. Throughout the time he worked there he was never informed about any specific expectations that needed to be met. Also, in the frequent meetings he had with his boss, no discussions had taken place about how he was doing and what he needed to improve. In the end, he just walked away with the awkward feeling that, the main reason why he had been fired, was the fact that he was not willing to pay for working. And that was peculiar, to say the least.

6 - THE ACCIDENTAL SUPERVISOR

THE CENSORED STORIES

A few years ago, a huge corporation, expanding their operations to Eastern Europe, found itself in desperate need to hire English speakers. As it is normal when a new organization is being built, many positions were available but there were not enough skilled candidates. The market was saturated with similar opportunities provided by other companies, which were also trying to get the job done by a cheaper workforce.

With such a competitive job market, HR had to take advantage of any initiatives that would get them the much needed candidates. A job fair was organized by local authorities and companies flocked to the event in the hope of finding qualified applicants that would fulfill the vacant positions.

Daniel was in Eastern Europe for different reasons: he was a sax player and loved to play his music in any venue that would be willing to pay for his performances. He was a middle-aged American, with an adventurous spirit and a bohemian life style. His laid back attitude and full dedication to his musical passion required, nonetheless, some regular income. Unfortunately, the money he earned on his occasional gigs was not enough to keep him afloat, so he decided to go with a friend to that same job fair.

His intention was to find some part-time work that would not interfere with his gigs. He had heard that English speakers were high on demand, so he thought that there was a strong possibility that he could find something to pay the bills. On his spare time, he would continue to thrill audiences with fabulous sax performances. At the job fair, they walked around the venue until they stopped by the corporation's stand. The HR clerks spoke enthusiastically about the available positions but Daniel showed little interest. His friend, however, urged him to pay attention to some of the jobs offered.

The keen eye of the HR lady spotted Daniel's lack of interest, so she decided to act boldly: *"Hey there!"* she called him, with a big smile on her face, *"I know that these are mostly entry level positions but would you be interested in a team supervisor role?"* Maybe it was the fact that he looked more mature than most applicants. Maybe it was his reserved approach and calm attitude. Whatever it was, the recruiter considered him as a potential candidate to a leadership role.

The truth was that Daniel had no experience in managing anything or anybody. The offer sounded attractive and the perspective of taking such job would certainly put an end to his money troubles.

"I'm sure it can't be that easy!" he thought to himself, while taking the seat offered by the sympathetic lady. He had no CV with him but a formal interview was agreed for the next day, at the company's office.

While going back to the flat that he shared with two of his friends, he couldn't stop thinking about the possibility of becoming a corporate employee. Most of all, he was surprised by how easy it all seemed to be. He had never had much luck in his life but this time it seems that things were changing. Back home in the US, with his background and experience, he wouldn't even be considered to a receptionist job, much less in a huge corporation like that one. But now, he was being invited to a role of supervisor, just because he was an American in foreign lands. *"It can't be that simple!"* he kept repeating to himself while entering the flat.

The following day came and Daniel decided to take it easy. He had a gig that evening, in a local cafe, and music was still his priority, so whatever happened with the interview, he had nothing to lose. He didn't really prepare the meeting since he had never been in a similar situation. Surely, he printed a copy of his CV, but the document only mentioned his musical experiences and the petty jobs that he had done in the past to keep his bills paid and to allow him to travel around the world.

The same HR lady, whom he had met in the job fair, started the interview. She was again very kind and helpful, making him feel at ease. She barely took a look at the CV and seemed to be more interested in his legal situation in the country. Also, she inquired if he had immediate availability to start working. Daniel answered all the questions with a smile, feeling that things were going better than he had expected. He learned that he would be interviewed by the operations manager, which would be the last step before the final decision was made.

After a few minutes of informal conversation, the HR lady left the meeting room, saying she would be right back with the manager. This gave Daniel some time to appreciate his surroundings: the company office was modern, full of glass walls and with an open space. From the room where he was seated he could see rows and rows of desks with people that seemed to be quite busy. The office was quite spacious and he had been told that all floors in the building were occupied by the company. More than three hundred people worked there. His thoughts were interrupted when a pleasant looking lady opened the door. The manager had arrived for his final interview.

What happened next, was beyond any of Daniel's wildest expectations. The lady had somewhat basic English and couldn't express herself properly. He managed to understand that she was the manager of the new organization and that the vacancy he was applying for was to supervise one of the most recent and bigger teams. It seemed that the previous supervisor had found a new job in the company, just a few months after joining it, so they were desperate for a replacement. Once again, the attention paid to his CV was minimum and the most important factor seemed to be that he was a native English speaker.

Apparently that was a huge advantage, since the team dealt frequently with their US colleagues.

Well, Daniel was a native speaker alright, but there was not much more that would make him a good fit for the job. Still he kept himself composed and smiled, trying to sound and look as formal as possible, even if he couldn't understand half of what the lady was saying. At some point, he even got the impression that she had no clue of what she was looking for, but he decided to keep that thought to himself.

Daniel left the interview with the promise of a very quick decision. He felt that the whole thing looked surreal and that, if he was offered the position, he would be getting himself into trouble. He decided to forget about the whole experience and try to get a part-time job, as he had initially planned.

Surprisingly, the offer came the next day: he had been hired and his monthly salary was way above the average in that country. Daniel hesitated. He had no idea how he would manage to deal with a boss that he could hardly understand but the money involved was too tempting to be refused. Against all expectations, the sax player was now a supervisor in a major global corporation.

He started work the following week. The first couple of days were spent with training and general overview about the company. After that, he was introduced to the team and was left alone. He soon learned that there were other supervisors in similar circumstances.

The whole environment seemed to be chaotic, with people left to fend for themselves and survive the best way they could. On the first team meeting, the impression that Daniel had formed during the interview was confirmed: the manager's conduct was of someone that was lost, trying to quickly fix things but in fact creating additional problems.

As for his own team members they ranked from those that were genuinely trying to get some work done and those that were spending their days watching movies on their computers, chatting around or playing music. Daniel's first corporate experience was a far cry from the stereotype that he had learned from the media or, more directly, from some of his friends, who worked in similar environments.

He tried the best he knew. Without clear guidance, having to rely on the advice of his own team members, he struggled to improve results and discipline the less productive. His knowledge of the business was poor and he was desperate for a promised trip to the US that would give him the know-how and contacts that he so badly needed. Either because there was such a poor organization or due to unavailability from those that should host him, the trip to the company's headquarters never materialized. Soon, Daniel became depressed and demotivated.

Inexperienced, with a clueless manager and little support from everyone else, Daniel was condemned from the start. Not only he felt lost in the chaotic setting of his office but music, his life's priority, was now being left behind. Running from one meeting to another, chasing people for answers that would never come, pressured for results that seemed unreachable, he decided to leave, a little more than a month after he accepted the job. His experience as a team manager had been a short one.

Daniel was replaced by someone else... and then by another. It took more than a year for the whole operation to settle and finally achieve the goals for which it had been created for. Importantly, his former manager also had to be replaced, to put an end to the chaos. Eventually, everything came into place and, a few years later, the operation was branded a success.

As to Daniel, soon he also got tired of the financial uncertainty that his passion for playing the sax brought to his life. He returned to the States, where he found a job as a second-hand car dealer, while at the same time he continued with his night gigs, playing in bars and restaurants. To this day, he still doesn't understand quite well what happened with his only corporate experience: was he hired by incompetent people? Or is it that getting that kind of job is just a matter of being at the right time in the right place? Probably, he will never know the answer to that question.

7 - SNIPERS AT THE OFFICE

THE CENSORED STORIES

The office space was brand new. Full of natural light, desks spread out through many square meters of pastel colored wooden floors surrounded by extravagantly decorated walls. With few private offices and a reasonable number of glass walled meeting rooms, the whole area transmitted an air of apparent transparency that the concept of "open office space" is keen to emphasize. The teams were scattered in islands of desk rows according to their functions and areas of business. All had been done to bring efficiency and sophistication together in one place.

The company itself was a rapidly expanding global e-commerce operation, with such levels of success that any long term planning was a difficult challenge. In fact, it was hard to keep up an organized seating plan as the teams were permanently hiring new people and desks had to be rearranged on a regular basis. A freshly inaugurated office was already becoming smaller by the day. On the opening ceremony the facilities team was congratulated by the CEO for the excellent job they had done and given the responsibility to plan an office extension.

One of these ever-growing teams was responsible for the logistics of the business. Like most of other departments they were busy not only with their increasing workload but also making sure that they had enough seats for new hires. At the same time, they were focused on a different priority: the company's very specific culture needed promoters and they were committed to be the champions of such an important duty.

The firm values were a mix of bold statements, with little or no practical meaning to people's daily life, and catchy phrases like "*Work hard, play hard*", that looked really cool to use in the employees email signatures. In the end, the overall idea was to make people believe that the environment was relaxed and that employees were *empowered* to bring their own (and the company's) development forward.

Immersed in this spirit, the logistics team members decided to show their pro-activeness in embracing the company values. After a chaotic brainstorming session, a decision was made that, they were sure, would bring a truly radical change to their daily routines. On the ground floor of the building they could regularly watch the IT guys playing online shoot-em-up games, but that seemed a little bit too nerdy for the logistics "action-driven" mentality. They needed something more lively, that would translate into the real world what their team was all about. They decided to buy plastic guns.

This way, to the joy of the logistic team members and the surprised faces of those surrounding them, suddenly the office was flooded by flying darts, fired from very colorful plastic guns. The guys would fiercely battle among themselves in every scheduled (or unscheduled) break they had, trying to "shoot" each other in successive waves of plastic bullets. Soon enough, members of other teams became either victims of such an intense snipping activity or had to buy similar weapons for purposes of "self-defense". Regardless of their function and their position, flying darts would democratically find their way into people's desks, computer monitors or even, occasionally, into people's faces. Everyone was an equal target in that war of the darts.

Undoubtedly, the initiative was a very original way to lift up the office morale and strengthen the team spirit, which is something that any self-respected corporation likes to achieve. It was true that some of the neighboring departments were not exactly thrilled with the idea of being targeted, by an unpredictable dart, while trying to carry on with their daily duties. However, the general opinion was that it was fun to be a part of a team with such a rebellious spirit and creative thinking. Still, not all was joy and laughter in the logistics world. There was another type of game that was widely practiced in the office and that no one dared to talk about: the art of deception.

Despite the relaxed and jovial approach, the obvious truth is that work had to be done. Lucas, the young energetic manager of the team, had his own criteria of what he thought were the ideal behaviors of a good employee. He wasn't concerned about all the flying darts and battlefield environment that, throughout the day, would engulf his team members. He would even shoot the occasional dart and laugh at being provocatively targeted by the plastic bullets. He was, nonetheless, keen in seeing regular displays of hard work and commitment from his employees. Or so he thought...

Every logistics team member knew the rules of the game and played it to the best of their abilities. Snipers with plastic guns, they were also specialists in another type of "snipping"! One that needed a specific type of "ammunition" to keep their boss happy. Indeed, they could afford to spend significant periods of their working hours playing and shooting around. However, the employees also understood that being the best sniper or, alternatively, working relentlessly eight hours of their shift wouldn't guaranty the good graces of their manager. Everybody knew that the key moment of their workday were the last ten minutes of their schedule.

At that crucial time of the day, all the playful behaviors would suddenly disappear and everyone would be sitting at their desks, typing furiously, pretending to be overwhelmed with work. Minutes would pass, the hour to leave the office would arrive, but nobody, from that team, would move an inch away from their desks. The big deception game was on.

People from other departments would gradually start

to leave. On their way out, while passing by the logistic team desks, they were met with apparent indifference. The occasional comment would be heard: "*Some people have good lives in this office!!*" whispered in a tone that was a mix of irony and victimization. Fifteen minutes after the hour, the next stage of the game would begin. With Lucas seating in his office, seemingly indifferent to his surroundings, heads would slowly start to turn around and people would look at each other, waiting to see who would be the first to break the lines.

Usually, after around half hour of overtime, a courageous (or desperate) soul would finally stand up and announce, with a worried expression:

"I'm full of work but I have to leave now or I won't catch my bus!"

A few heads would nod in agreement! Others, with a much more ingenious mind, would just pack up and, sighing heavily, express their intention of "*working during the evening to catch up with the backlog*". After the departure of the first team member, others would follow, in a mournful procession, many often displaying exhausted expressions or concerned looks. The most cunning of all would hold on until the boss decided to go home. This usually meant staying one additional hour of overtime. Their moment of glory finally arrived: Lucas, with a hardly disguised tone of guilt in his voice, would wish them a good evening and suggest that they should go home too.

The reality is that everyone on that team knew that

the manager evaluated their performance by the time that they spent in the office after the shift ended. Depending on how regular and visible would their *"overtime commitment"* be, the more chances they had of getting the performance bonus that was paid every six months.

Employees also understood that doing a good job during regular working hours would not be enough to secure the bonus. The daily performance of the "overtime game" was mandatory. Eventually, this lead to low productivity levels during the normal working hours, since they all felt the *"need"* to stay late. The plastic guns were just a way to keep them busy until the real daily performance evaluation would happen.

Like in many other aspects of corporate life, the sniper game was nothing but a mask hiding an aspect that is present in the culture of most multinational corporations: *"more important than what you do, it's what you appear to be doing."* Lucas was happy to have his team displaying the energetic and "out-of-the-box" behaviors the company encouraged them to cultivate. It was good for his image, putting him on the front-line of a very competitive leadership team.

However, in Lucas's view, no plastic guns in the world would be enough, unless employees would regularly be willing to stay after their shift ended. This was, from the manager's perspective, the only true evidence of commitment and hard work. As a result, he was willing to reward those that did it and forget the few that didn't comply.

Lucas's wasn't alone in his way of thinking. Other manager's imitated his approach and soon the "game of deception" was played by other teams. In the meantime, his career progressed fast: he became a director and then vice-president in less than 3 years. Some of his former colleagues progressed fast as well. Others got tired of the daily theater and just left the company. Apparently, they weren't able to improve their acting skills or shooting abilities. Poor souls.

8 - MENTORING FOR IDIOTS

The manager was not in his best mood. He was again participating in one of those talent development programs that only gave him extra work and little reward. It was the second time, in consecutive years, that he had been selected to be one of the attendants. In other circumstances, this would be a reason to make him proud, as it clearly proved that he was being recognized as someone with great potential within the company. But he knew better..

Talent development programs are regular occurrences in major corporations. In theory, their goal is to help identify and promote the talent that exists within the company and to provide additional knowledge that can help bring your career forward. In reality, it's mostly an activity that gives extra workload to those involved and contributes very little to increase the chances of getting a promotion.

This program started with a trip aimed at getting all participants together. The talented employees and their mentors were given the opportunity to meet each other, face to face, for the first time. The initial meeting brought them all to one of the company sites in the UK. When everyone was comfortably sitting in a large room, introductions took place, followed by some formal inaugural speeches. People looked relaxed and smiley, trying to make the best of the change in their daily routines. After a break for refreshments, the mentors presented some generic slides about the program and the steps that needed to be followed.

Still, the gathering was mostly focused on people getting to know each other. This meant that most of the program consisted in enjoying abundant meals and fine entertainment. A relaxed atmosphere in a British pub, with local lager and fine cuisine made wonders to improve the team spirit. Unfortunately, on the next day, the trip was cut short by a fire in the office. While the firemen did their job, the group met for a last time in the building's parking lot. Even when a fire occurs, it's business as usual and, after a brief farewell, everyone went straight to the airport, with a number of tasks to complete over the following months.

On that specific day, the manager had to deal with one of those tasks. As part of the activities of the program, he would have a first call with his mentor who, for business reasons, had failed to show up in the initial meeting. One of the guidelines of the program stated that:

"Talent development can only be achieved by direct interaction with the company's senior leadership"

That meant, in this case, a monthly call between mentor and apprentice, with the honorable goal of providing guidance and knowledge sharing.

His mentor was a senior director who worked in a different division, in another building. He was a complete stranger to the manager and this made him a bit nervous as he didn't know what to expect from him. At the agreed time, the call begun with the usual polite introductions. The manager´s first impressions of his mentor were positive: his approach sounded laid back, without any hint of arrogance or patronizing attitude. After the first five minutes of informal conversation the director decided to get down to business:

"So, would you like to make a career in this company?" he asked.

Although sudden, the frank question had some logic as that program was, basically, aimed at those that would eventually escalate the career ladder. The manager hesitated at first but eventually gave his answer:

"Well, I don't have any major ambitions. I think I would settle for a director position in the future, but I don't aspire to anything higher than that."

There was some sort of silence on the other side of the line, until the sharp voice of the director was heard, with another question:

"And what do you intend to do to get there?"

The manager replied with the trivial corporate template sentences such as:

"...that he would rise through hard work, delivering the required results and contributing to the development of the organization, bla, bla, bla...".

To his surprise, he soon realized that his mentor was laughing at the reply.

Trying to control the laughter, while the astonished manager on the other side of the line wondered why his reply was so funny, the director finally regained his composure and replied:

"No, you got it all wrong. Listen, it doesn't take me long to identify an intelligent and articulated person. You are clearly one of them so my only advise for you is to leave the company!"

The manager was so surprised, that he was unable to say anything for a while.

"I know these are not the words you were expecting to listen from me" - he proceeded - *"but please, let me explain: to rise in the career ladder you have to be an idiot with a good network. Higher leadership is full of idiots that drink their coffee with the right people and they don't like to see intelligent folks like you going up and mingling around. It may spoil their arrangements, you see! So... if you want to progress, either you become one of them or you just have to leave the company".*

Feeling encouraged by the sincerity and straightforwardness of the director, the manager made the only obvious question that he could think of at that moment:

"But...you are a senior director so... are you calling yourself an idiot as well?"

The mentor laughed again:

"No! Actually, I just left the division where you work and came to this one, because here the concentration of idiots is not as big as in your business!"

The manager was struggling to understand the full meaning of what he had just heard. There he was, in a call with one of the company's senior leaders, telling him that all the leadership was a bunch of idiots. He tried to clarify:

"But how come idiots get to leadership positions? That would bring the collapse of the company, wouldn't it?"

With a more serious tone on his voice, the director replied:

"Look, let me be as clear as possible. The company won't collapse as long as there are competent managers and lower rank employees doing the work for the idiots. There are several reasons why idiots get promoted faster and usually that's linked with their ability to network and get friends in the right places. When it's their turn to be on top of the ladder they realize that all others are like them. So the big chiefs only need to pretend to be smart and get the proper people to do their job for them. Simple. The fact that they are idiots doesn't necessarily mean that they are stupid."

The call ended shortly after this last statement and the manager took some minutes to think on what he had just heard. Somehow this was the best and the worst mentor he could ever imagine. Best because he had been brutally honest and much of what he said matched the manager's own opinion of his work environment. Worst because, through his straightforwardness, he was pushing people out of the company, which was the opposite of what a mentor should be doing. Regardless of this contradictory feelings, that rare moment of down-to-earth honesty made the manager´s day.

The program progressed and the director and the manager had their regular calls, which were always taking place in a spirit of open and frank dialogue. Nonetheless, the content of those discussions was never shared outside of those meetings. Their conversations were the highlight of the manager's mentoring program. At the same time he worked hard to complete his assigned project: to increase the sales revenue of his own department. After long hours and weekend overtime a process was designed and put in place that could, potentially, increase sales by 10%. His project was an instant success and compliments came from all the leaders involved.

In the last gathering, organized to celebrate the completion of the program, his mentor was not able to attend, this time due to personal reasons. In the end, they never got to meet in person.

In fact, the future would prove that the words of that

mentor were closer to the reality than the manager would have ever imagined! One year after the talent development program ended, the sales department in the same division where he worked, failed to reach quarterly targets. As a consequence, the leadership decided to enforce a strict control of all expenses, resulting in almost five hundred people losing their jobs. This was how the company *calibrated* the failure of the sales reps in achieving the forecasted revenue. At the same time, the all so important Wall Street investors were pleased with the outcome, as the projected profits growth was assured. Interestingly, none of those people fired worked for the sales department.

The manager was one of the victims. Despite his success in achieving results and after two consecutive talent development programs completed with distinction, it was time for the company to throw one of his rising stars off the window, to the care of unemployment services. His successful project was also scrapped. His teams reached all targets and objectives but that didn't prevent him from suffering the consequences of the failures of another department.

He took it gracefully, his only regret being that he had not followed one of the advises of the mentor: he didn't manage to have coffee with the right people, at the right time. Improving his caffeine drinking habits was now decisive to be able to succeed in his future career.

9 - THE CASE OF THE SLEEPY ENGINEER

THE CENSORED STORIES

Karel was working as a customer service agent in a big multinational company. He got his job like many others at the time: the company decided to open an operation in a less expensive country and, since English speaking candidates were lacking, he decided to give it a try. The selection process was fast and after only one interview he got the job. It was true that Karel's CV was not 100% accurate, but he saw nothing wrong in exaggerating his experience.

Previously he had done something similar. Taking things a bit too far, he managed to convince a school in Taiwan that he was a *"certified native English teacher"*. He was neither certified or a native English speaker but his boldness paid off and he managed to teach English to young Taiwanese for over two years. In the process, he learned a bit of Mandarin and traveled around Asia, fulfilling one of his childhood dreams.

Back in his home country, Karel wasn't doing particularly well as a customer support agent. His productivity was low, he was not committed to the tasks and he made many mistakes. He saw his job has a gateway to other possibilities in the corporate ladder but he wasn't willing to put the effort. His dream was to get a position that would allow him to travel and see the world. Anyway, he wasn't obsessed about it and, deep inside, believed that things would happen naturally.

Outside of the office, his priority was to party relentlessly. The little money he made in his corporate job was used to pay the bills and get him drunk or stoned (or both) almost every night. Eventually this lifestyle contributed to his poor performance at work. Long nights without rest took an unavoidable toll on him and, occasionally, Karel would be caught at his desk deeply asleep, with his mouth open, almost falling of the chair.

So far he had been able to get away with his behavior. Partially, he felt secure because a lot of his colleagues quit the job after a few months, so anyone that showed willingness to stay in the long term was appreciated. Supervisors and managers tolerated low productivity and poor quality coming from some employees just to assure stability and avoid the need to go into yet another recruitment process. In any circumstance, Karel's performance wasn't that bad and his supervisor still believed that, if he partied a little less, his productivity would improve.

Teams were regularly getting new duties and responsibilities. As part of this permanently changing environment, Karel was transferred to a different group, where his skills seemed to be in demand. With that move he also got a new boss, which, from the start, appeared to be less supportive and not too keen in shutting the eyes to Karel's obvious shortcomings. His productivity was checked more than ever and his unruly behavior was not overlooked any more. His new supervisor wanted him to be an example to the rest of the team, since he was one of the more seasoned agents in the platform.

Suddenly, his short corporate career seemed to be close to an end. Not happy with the lack of progress from Karel's side, his new manager decided to take action. After a few meetings, the supervisor confronted him with a plan that would assure that his performance would improve. Basically, the plan was made of a set of tasks and goals that needed to be completed in a short period of time. The company had a name to this sort of plans. They were called P.I.P's, the fancy acronym for performance improvement plan. HR got involved, a document was signed by both parties and all was done with a sense of formality. Everyone knew, though, that the P.I.P. was frequently the last stop before the exit door was shown.

Karel reacted to all this with the serenity of those that know that luck is on their side. He accepted the P.I.P. as a challenge and actually thought that the targets were not that difficult to achieve. For a while, he attended less parties and managed to stay focused on his daily tasks. At the same time, he decided to apply (internally) for another job: quality engineer. The fact that he was not an engineer seemed to be secondary and the detail that he knew very little (or nothing) about quality was nothing more than an irrelevant triviality.

Once again, he exaggerated his CV, knowing that it would be a different HR department handling his application. He didn't technically lie when he said that his currently daily job was connected to engineering and that quality was very important on his day-to-day tasks. In reality he did have contact with the company's engineers (once in a while) and there was a strict quality control on the job that he was doing. What he *"neglected"* to mention was the fact that he was regularly failing those quality checks which had been one of the reasons why he was currently on a P.I.P.

To everyone's surprise (Karel included), his application progressed. HR didn't screen the forged CV and forwarded it to the hiring managers. Interviews were made, most of them over the phone, and he was able to reach the final stage of the recruitment process. At that point, the engineer's director contacted Karel's boss and asked for feedback. A call was setup and the supervisor provided an honest evaluation, mentioning all the shortcomings of his employee. To his surprise, the director dismissed all concerns and drawbacks described by his colleague. Instead, he insisted in all the advantages that Karel's application had for the role: *"After all, he is a local so, therefore, more reliable. He will also be much cheaper than external candidates and this is a big plus!"* The call ended and the supervisor could hardly believe in what he had just heard.

Needless to say Karel got the job. The big multinational company had a new quality engineer. One that was foreign to quality and oblivious of engineering. He was cheap and reliable and that was enough to override his drawbacks for the role. The P.I.P. became redundant and the new engineer moved to the upper floor of the building, where the more technically knowledgeable teams were based. His triumph was absolute and he couldn't keep himself from celebrating with another memorable party, that lasted all night long.

Still hardly believing that he had managed to get the job, Karel quickly settled in his new functions. He was working on his own and although the new colleagues were not exactly welcoming, he enjoyed the fact that he had no boss checking him all the time. The new tasks at hand seemed more complicated than he initially predicted but, with his unshakable confidence, he knew he would get there.

Karel was a person of habits and routines. As soon as the novelty passed, he returned to the same old ways that had got him into trouble in the first place. The job was complicated, required a lot of networking and analytical skills. His time was spent trying to get answers from other departments or going through piles of documents and files. Reports and detailed analysis were being asked all the time. Combining this type of work with a lifestyle of partying and boozing wasn't exactly easy. Soon enough he was again being caught, by some of his work colleagues, dozing in at his desk or barely being able to keep his eyes open.

A few months later, he committed a major blunder. The analysis he made of an important case was incorrect and the report useless. Some weeks later the same happened and his boss gave him an ultimatum: either he would get his act together or he would be fired. Karel struggled, but he was still confident that he could make it. His colleagues were now aware of his lack of knowledge and were keen to point that out to his boss. His promotion was not going as planned.

Time passed and he managed to stay afloat until one day, when a senior vice-president made a stopover in the office. While making the traditional visit to all floors in the building, the senior leader passed by the row of desks where Karel was usually seating. To everyone's amazement, in one of the desks, our hero was seating, with the head tilted backwards and the mouth open, producing a snoring sound that could hardly go undetected. The vice-president glanced at him, with an appalled expression, and carried on with the visit.

Karel's destiny was decided on that day. As soon as the news came to the knowledge of his manager, he was fired without any delay. He had lasted almost one year as a quality engineer. Most people would have felt devastated but Karel took it quite well. He knew that this experience had been an invaluable one and he could now apply to other quality engineer jobs without even having to forge his CV.

The company would have now the opportunity to correct the mistake and hire a qualified person for the job. That would be what common sense and logic would dictate. Karel was quickly replaced by another internal candidate. This time it was somebody that had been working for a while in a quality department, so from that perspective, it matched the criteria. Still, the new quality engineer was as foreign to engineering as Karel was. The CV had also been forged and the skills inflated. As it seems, the lessons of a recent past had not been totally learned.

10 - THE KINKY DIRECTOR

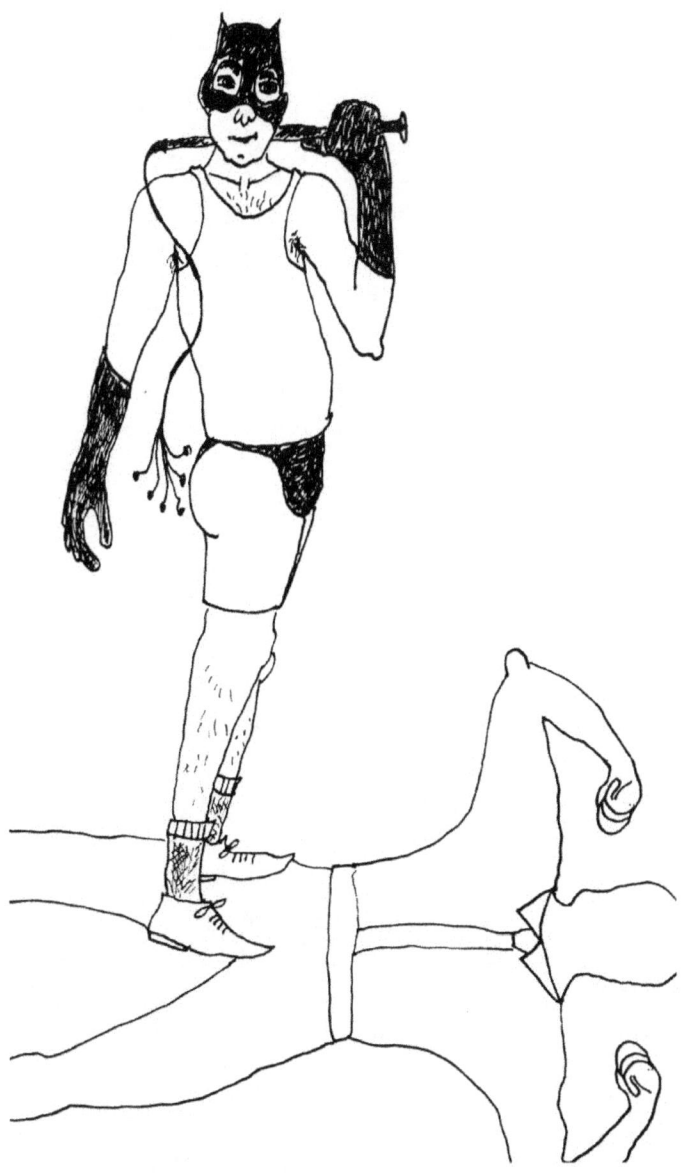

It was hard to rise in the career ladder of this particular corporation. Sometimes it could be just a matter of luck. Other times you would have to be in the right place at the right time. Most of the times, it was just a question of pleasing the right people. For Bert, none of this had happened: he was still trying to get himself above his current level as a manager.

A recent move that he had pushed for, sending him to a different department, seemed promising at first but once again things were slowing down and his new team didn't seem to have either the size or the experience to propel his career forward.

Nonetheless, Bert was not of the type of person that would give up easily. He kept investing in his professional network and tried to socialize as much as possible within the office premises and even outside of them. The regular team building events were excellent occasions to increase his visibility and provide the necessary contacts that could be useful in future career steps. The leadership changes were quite common and he wanted to be prepared in case an opportunity would come up. The more known he was, the bigger were his chances.

The winds began to change when his boss was replaced by a new senior director. The new guy seemed to be quite approachable and open to support the career ambitions of his direct reports. Bert made it very clear from the beginning that he thought that his current position was worthy of a director title. Furthermore, he would see a promotion as a deserved recognition for his hard work in the department. Modesty and restraint weren't Bert's strongest qualities.

Months passed and Bert's message was repeated over and over again. At every opportunity he would bring the topic forward, enumerating the reasons why recognition of his efforts would be more than deserved. His boss slowly got tired of listening the same speech after every meeting and decided it was time to do something about it. Due to finance restrictions, he had no authorization to promote any more of his direct reports. He had mentioned this several times to Bert but his argument seemed to have no effect on Bert's crusade to get himself promoted. A middle ground solution had to be found.

Although outside of the rules, companies usually allow leaders to use some "tricks" that can keep those that are "overly ambitious" satisfied... at least for a while. Whiners are usually unpopular among corporate ranks, but Bert was delivering the required results so his refusal to take no for an answer was somehow tolerated. Therefore, the senior director presented the interim solution that he thought would appease Bert: he would be able to call himself a director, he would be able to use the title in his professional interaction with colleagues but... he wouldn't get the pay grade and the benefits of the job. At least, not just yet.

Bert was not entirely satisfied with this proposal, especially because his ambitions were also of a financial nature, but the fact that he could make use of the pompous title of director was enough to bring a smile to his face. He took no time in changing his signature and announcing it to everybody he knew in the office, including naturally, his own team members. There was this little annoyance that his true rank as manager would still appear on the company system profile (this would only change when he would really get the position) but that was not enough to make him less proud of his achievement.

Carried away by the excitement, Bert decided to walk around every single corner of the office, visiting both floors of the glass walled building. With his small figure (but a pompous attitude), he could hardly go unnoticed, walking between rows of desks, breezing quickly through the open office area. In fact, his presence was being mostly ignored. Just some heads would turn, with an enquiring expression, trying to understand why that curious character was walking around them.

His triumphant display was so pleasant to him that he decided to make it a daily habit. He was not the highest ranked manager in the office, but he couldn't hold himself and, soon enough, his *"inspection of the troops"* became a routine. Seeing Bert, *the director*, walking around by the end of the day, became a trivial event in that company. Life was smiling to the new appointed director and he was enjoying every minute of it. However, an unexpected turn of events would soon bring clouds to this happy scenario.

Frequent business traveling was an important part of Bert's responsibilities. He either visited prospective clients or attended the all so important leadership meetings. He was keen on those trips for several reasons, but one of the most significant was the opportunity to share his new gained position with peers and customers. Infused by his refreshed sense of importance, his trips were now an extension of his triumphant daily walks. During one of these business travels he spent a full week out of the office. He had to visit several locations and was so busy that he wasn't able to keep his emails under control, so slowly a backlog grew up.

One of the unattended emails concerned a request for a specific sales report. It wasn't urgent but he had to deliver it till the end of the week. In the office, Bert's team had the usual weekly meeting with senior leadership and the lack of the report became an issue. The senior director mentioned that Bert had already finished the report but he hadn't sent it yet. Unable to reach his boss, as he was flying one of those long transatlantic flights, one of Bert's account managers decided to take action.

Fueled by an increasing sense of urgency and by the opportunity to please leadership, the account manager had an idea: what if the boss had kept the report in his office! If so, it would be just a matter of scanning it and sending it to the right audience. His *director* would be extremely grateful and he would be rewarded for his pro-activity. Luckily, Bert had left the office unlocked, so the manager began the search immediately.

Bert's office was organized, with a Spartan tidiness that reflected perfectly the personality of its occupier. One of the shelves was quickly searched with no results. On the desk, some paperwork was neatly placed in a tray marked with an *"Urgent"* label. Bert was old-fashioned: if it was urgent, he had to print it and make notes on how he would address the issue. However, the report was not there either. *"Damn!"* cursed the employee *"Where did he put it?"* Only one place was left: the drawers of his desk. Usually they were left locked, especially if the office tenant would be outside of the office. Surprisingly, the key was on the lock and it had not been used. Breathing deeply, he decided to take a look.

The first two drawers revealed nothing but some personal belongings, an agenda and even some money, mostly coins. The third (and bigger drawer) was the last one to be opened and it revealed an awkward set of objects. Among those items the most notorious was a whip. A black leather whip. Next to it, carefully folded, was a black latex suit. Underneath the suit and the whip, an exquisite set of magazines devoted to the thematic of sadomasochism. Shocked by his findings, the employee closed the drawers and left the office. The report was quickly forgotten and Bert's reputation had suffered irreparable damage.

Office gossip is one of the unavoidable components of corporate life. As a communication channel, is faster than any other means available in the office. As a creator of rumors is absolutely ruthless. The story with the content of the drawer in Bert's desk spread like wildfire. Different versions circulated and bizarre elements were added like the one that speculated that he walked around the office to search for people that would be the subject of his colored fantasies.

When Bert returned from his business trip, he rapidly noticed the bemused looks and hardly hidden giggles that would follow him wherever he would go. First he thought it was just his impression but then it became so obvious that he had to admit that something had happened in his absence. When he finally realized that he had left his desk drawers unlocked, reality struck and he felt crushed by the possibility that the whole office would know about his particular tastes.

Most people would be so overwhelmed with embarrassment that they would quit their jobs or, at least, hide themselves from the world. Not Bert, though. Yes, he felt his self-confidence had been shaken and his authority undermined. Nonetheless, he was determined and was hardly the type of person that gives up easily. After a few days of restraint, he returned to his usual work routines, with an air of defiance and absolute resolution.

The only difference was that now his daily walks were

done in a faster pace and he would try to avoid the staring looks of some of his colleagues. He also displayed a less firm hand with his own team members to avoid conflicts and make sure that the story would not reach anyone outside of the office walls. Bert was still going to make his career go forward, no matter what, and office rumors would certainly not prevent him from fulfilling his professional ambitions.

Bert didn't progress much in the following years. He finally became a real director but not a lot happened after that. The office suffered many changes, people came and left to the point that it was hard to keep up with who was doing what. The daily walks came to an end as Bert's career came to a standstill. His ambition was still there but the opportunities were now fewer and less attractive.

Sometimes, at the end of the day, when the building was almost empty, Bert would sit in his office and open the last drawer of his desk. It was now filled in with papers and files that he no longer needed. It had once been filled with a different type of content. Bert wondered if his colleague's vision of him, dressed in a latex suit, with a whip on his hand, was what kept him from moving forward on his corporate career. He would never know.

11 - EVALUATION FOR DUMMIES

THE CENSORED STORIES

"*What does a recruiter from HR and a financial analyst have in common?*" asked one of the newly appointed supervisors in that team.

"*Well, they work in the same company and apparently they do a good job.*" replied her counterpart, trying not to sound too patronizing.

"*Yes, I know that but why we should be comparing their performance? Why are we discussing which one of them is better to find out who gets the best bonus?*" insisted the supervisor, with an expression of confusion in her face.

Those were questions that her colleague was not ready to answer. Not at that point. They had been made supervisors just 6 months ago and it was the first time that they were handling the annual performance review of their own team members. They had some Bell curve system implemented to help with the evaluation, but it all seemed too complicated.

"Let's go and talk to our boss. He worked with this type of systems before, I'm sure he can clarify most of our doubts", one of them said.

Their manager was a seasoned leader, with extensive experience in several companies. He was always ready to support his employees, particularly those with less maturity on their roles. That was the case of the supervisors that he had recently appointed to one of his teams. They were very talented, energetic and hard-working employees, but they still needed to develop their leadership skills and self-confidence for the new positions they now held.

He was not surprised when they requested a meeting to discuss the evaluation system. That was a topic that he struggled to deal with, even with all his past experience. It was not that the rules and the processes were difficult to follow. No, that could be learned in an afternoon. It was the principle that was difficult to understand. He was convinced that the reason why many companies used those evaluation systems was that they simply didn't trust their managers. The assumption was that, without such system in place, the managers wouldn't be able to perform an honest and fair assessment of their employee's performance.

"Look, I'm not going to withhold anything back from you", he said at the beginning of the meeting with his supervisors. *"I want you to have all the information possible to help you go through this exercise, since its one of the most relevant duties that you have. Don't forget that you are dealing with people's salaries and that's the most important thing for*

any employee."

Both supervisors had now their notebooks open and were fully focused on the words of their boss.

"Let me explain why many companies have this type of systems in place. Nobody else will ever tell you this but the reason is simple: the company doesn't trust us. The truth is that, in the past, managers were too biased when conducting evaluations. They either gave their team members great scores because they wanted to be popular or they would favor some employees versus others, making the whole evaluation a subjective exercise. Basically, people were not happy with the result and companies were not happy to see such random behaviors in their managers. So they decided to create some rules.

"Why didn't they just replace the managers or gave them some training so they could do better evaluations?" one of the supervisors interrupted.

"Excellent question!" the boss replied. *"You see, companies thought that, by imposing some rules, they would get the managers to have a similar approach to performance reviews. This would result in fairer evaluations and happier employees. On the other hand, it would not be wise for a corporation to admit that they had hired managers that were incapable of treating employees fairly so...it was easier to take the task out of their hands than firing them."*

"So... you are saying that this "curve system" takes the responsibility of evaluating people from us?" inquired one of the supervisors, while the other was scribbling notes on a sheet of paper.

"Well, not completely but you certainly don't "own" the process. Lets put it this way: a freshman out university gets his first job in a big company like ours. That person will think that if he works hard, meets or even exceeds the targets setup on him and become a great team member, the company will compensate him for the good performance with a wonderful pay rise by the end of the year. Unfortunately, that's not exactly what happens. The system will determine if that performance can be compensated... or not."

"So, basically, the employee's evaluation is not fairer with this system in place? That's what you are saying, right?"

"Exactly", the manager replied. *"What is the system anyway? I know you received a load of emails explaining it and we've discussed this before, but let me put it as simple as possible."*

In this moment he approached the white board in the meeting room, acting like a teacher that was about to give a lesson to his pupils:

"The rules differ from company to company, but the basics are as follows" he said, while scribbling in the board. *"First, an average percentage of pay rise is established for all employees. Usually this is a low figure as companies don't like to raise salaries. Lets say its 3%. This means that, right from the start, most employees will have to be on this 3% salary increase range. The really good ones will receive a bit more... let's say 4% and the ones under-performing get less or even no pay rise. The idea behind all this is to make sure that the majority of the workers gets a rise under "control", regardless of their performance."*

"But then we have the quotas..." interrupted one of the

supervisors.

"Precisely! That's the key ingredient of the evaluation system. It decides how many good employees you have and even how many bad employees you have. So, in your team of 10 people, the system tells that you can have 3 top performers and 2 low performers. The rest falls into the average. These are the rules and you can't run away from them. For example: if you have 4 people in your team who are really good, you will have to let one down because of the quotas. That's not really fair, is it? Even worst: lets say that you don't have any bad performer in your team. Still, you will have to put 2 team members on that category. That's even more unjust as these people won't get any pay rise and their evaluation won't match their real performance! Not exactly motivating, is it?"

He noticed the dismayed expressions in supervisor's faces but still he pressed forward:

"Yes, but you were also told that the system is so good that even allows specific individual compensations, according to people's performance. This means that not everyone in the same range will get the same pay rise. For example, the average folks that will be getting 3% will be ranked, so that some get 3.1%, others 3.4% and so on. The reality, however, is that there is almost no difference in their salaries when they get paid. It's just to pretend that everybody gets a proper evaluation, but in the end, it's all very controlled. The funny part is that you will have to present the performance review to your employees without even mentioning any of these rules. Not an easy task, I can tell you that."

"And what about this comparison of our teams with other departments in the office? It doesn't make any sense to me!"

inquired the supervisor, with an intrigued expression."

"Ah, the famous office leveling. You see, the quotas don't apply only to individual teams. They also can be applied to a location with different departments, which is our case. This means that the entire office can only have a given share or percentage of good, average and bad performers. I'll write down our quotas for this year"

- 30% of good performers
- 50% of average performers
- 20% of bad performers

"That's why you are meeting with the supervisors from the other departments to reach an agreement on those percentages. The discussions can easily turn into bizarre conversations."

"And that's why we requested this meeting. We can't understand why we should be comparing the performance of our guys with people that do something completely different. It doesn't make any sense to us!" ranted one of the supervisors, letting some steam out.

"Unfortunately, I know what you are talking about. Usually managers want to compensate their good employees and when there is a restriction on how many good performers an office can have, things can get nasty. The idea is to have a fair distribution of the quotas between different teams but the result is that you end up comparing apples and onions."

"Yeah, yesterday we witnessed an argument between the HR manager and one of the leaders of the finance team for a place among the top performers! They were almost arguing to convince each other, and everyone else, of the merits of their respective

employees. Suddenly we had to decide if a HR recruiter was doing a better job than a financial analyst. It was surreal!!" – confessed the supervisor, letting some additional steam off.

"You will have to learn how to deal with it. If you reveal the whole truth to the employees they may have some issues to understand it as well. That's why this whole system is fundamentally subjective and fails to deliver the fair treatment promised. In the end, the logic of good workers getting the reward that they deserve is lost in the labyrinth of company policies. Getting a pay rise can depend on how convincing your supervisor can be when meeting other managers. That's something an employee would find highly demotivating, right? Nonetheless, these are the rules of the game and we have to play it."

The meeting ended shortly afterwards, with the overwhelmed supervisors reflecting on their new responsibilities and on how would they handle the difficult task of communicating results to team members. They had one additional meeting with other departments and generically speaking, they did quite well defending their own evaluation of their employees. Only one battle was lost, when an additional spot in the top performers list was finally given to someone from another team, based on the argument that *"he arrives early to work in the morning"*.

The supervisor left that meeting with the hard task of telling her team member that she had not been chosen for a top performer spot because she *didn't* arrive early enough to the office. Quite motivating indeed!

12 - A POCKET FULL OF MONEY

THE CENSORED STORIES

François was the account manager of one of the company's biggest clients. The job was good, he was able to do most of his work independently and had a quite flexible time schedule. His account was very important but, at the same time, it didn't give him much trouble. Ultimately, he found himself quite often getting bored at work and even if he had never been a career person, it crossed his mind that maybe it was the right time to try to do something else.

The opportunities in his organization were not that many. He had a good network with those that he cooperated with on a regular basis, but that was not enough to fast track him into a different position. Divided between the increased feeling of a dead-end and the fear of leaving his comfort zone, he nonetheless started to look for job vacancies outside of his own department.

In one of these searches, he bumped into an internal newsletter that publicized a job as Senior Customer Support Manager. The position was appealing as it would mean a promotion but at the same time, it was a field that was far from prestigious, with little relevance within the company hierarchy. He was about to discard this possibility when he noticed the place where the customer support operation was based in: the capital of an Eastern Europe country.

He had traveled several times to Eastern Europe, both for business as well as for leisure. This was not a case of someone particularly fascinated with the architecture and history of that part of Europe. What appealed to him was a different type of beauty: Slavic girls. He was well known (he had never denied it himself) for having more than a soft spot for the fair sex. On top of that, ladies from that part of the continent were not only beautiful but also they were, in his experience, more accessible than the ones back home.

François, our Account Program Manager, left the office that day dwelling with the opposite feelings that he had about the position. However, deep inside, he had already decided to give it a try. The shortcomings of the job were not enough to override the excitement he felt by the thought that he could be soon surrounded by Slavic ladies, working on a daily basis with him. That became engraved in his mind. On the other hand, François knew that, even if things didn't work out well in this new position, doors would always be open for him to return back to his old job. He was a reliable employee and his boss would take him back anytime.

As the recruitment process progressed, his commitment and enthusiasm increased as well. After several interviews, including one with a visit to his future office, he finally got the job. His success came with two (unexpected) extra bonuses: he actually didn't need to relocate to the city where the operation was based. A monthly visit would be enough and he would be allowed to manage teams remotely the rest of the time. This made the logistics of relocating easier. The other unexpected advantage was that he would co-manage the operation with a well-known colleague who also had been hired recently. They shared a similar background and both seemed to be keen in pushing their careers forward. His new position was off to a great start.

Soon he met his new teams and colleagues. His expectations were not defrauded: the office was a mix of foreigners and local citizens, with a vast majority of ladies of Slavic origin. He felt that life was being kind to him. François was aware that he had not been born with the most attractive physical traits. Every time he woke up in the morning, he understood that it would not be his gallant looks that would bring him into favor with the attractive ladies surrounding him. But he was well spoken, a foreigner in a country where that feature was an advantage in the eyes of the opposite sex and most of all, he was the boss. Our newly appointed Senior Manager knew very well the powerful effect that his new position had on those that worked with him. He was certain that his status had the potential to make his new job a memorable one, in many sort of ways. Or so he thought.

His first visits produced another positive reassurance: he and the other manager clicked wonderfully, like if old friends had been reunited. They also soon found out that there was already a lot of competence and knowledge on their newly given operation, so their job was cut out for them. All they had to do was to keep things going on smoothly and ensure a long-term future for all the teams that were now reporting to them. François even managed to act discreetly and without too much effort, started to get signs of sympathy from some of the ladies in the office, including one of his direct reports.

Months passed and although he tried to behave as professional as possible, he found himself unable to resist temptation. Soon enough he was having occasional adventurous encounters with a restricted number of his female colleagues. He made sure that nothing of his *extracurricular activities* would be known but unavoidably, his womanizing side became part of the local office gossip. However, François didn't spend enough time in the office to be directly exposed to such rumors and there was no evidence of professional wrongdoing. His career move was a complete success and had met all of his wildest expectations.

Nonetheless, there was a particular girl that had caught his attention. She was not only beautiful, but also her reputation indicated that she would be an accessible target. He discretely made some inquiries about her and found out that, apparently, she was desperate to find a nice well-to-do gentleman. François thought that his profile matched perfectly with her expectations. He tried some timid advances, without any visible results. The occasional conversations he had with her didn't match at all the reputation that the girl was told to have. To make matters worse, she had recently delivered her resignation from the company and her termination period was already close to an end.

Our senior manager felt that he had to act quickly to make sure that, once more, he would achieve his very own personal goals. The urgency of the situation required a less conservative approach than usual, so he planned his next move carefully. First, he told the lady's supervisor that he would take care of her employee's exit interview. The excuse was that he would like to listen, first-hand, why people were leaving the company and what could be done, in the future, to make them stay. Then, he booked the interview to a more discreet meeting room, at a time when most people would have already left for the day. Most shifts ended at 5PM, so he made sure the meeting would take place half an hour later. If everything would go as planned, he would invite her for a drink, after the interview was over.

The day arrived and François took some extra care with his appearance: he made sure he was wearing one of his best suits, combed his hair and trademark mustache and finally, he even sprayed himself generously with an extra dose of his favorite "*eau-de-toilette*". The day dragged itself with the usual duties and, as the hours slowly passed, François had more and more difficulties in hiding his excitement with the meeting and what might happen afterwards. The scheduled time finally arrived and, while walking to the meeting room, an idea popped up to his mind: he decided to use one additional convincing argument, in case his position and natural charm wouldn't be enough to seduce his lady colleague. Discreetly, he pulled some money out of his wallet and placed it strategically on the front pocket of his jacket. With just the tip of the bills visible, François felt an additional boost of confidence that would certainly, he thought, guaranty a successful result to their meeting.

The girl was already seated and waiting when he arrived to the room. It was one of the smallest meeting rooms in the office, ensuring a close proximity. Brimming with self confidence, the manager opened the conversation with an informal tone trying to make a relaxing and friendly environment. The lady replied with courtesy and even a timid smile, indicating that all seemed to be going according to François plan.

He tried everything, even offering a promotion in case she would stay in the company. When he got no reaction, he also offered all his support in case she would need references to continue her career elsewhere. He used his best smile, the smoothest words he could find and several times indicated, without being too obvious, the direction of his pocket, where the money was still visible. To all this she reacted with thankfulness but refusing all offers and with no encouraging signs.

Drops of sweat slowly formed in the manager's forehead. The room was small, he could feel the proximity of her presence, seating in front of him, with an expression of calmness throughout the conversation. He felt increasingly uncomfortable and started to have doubts about his approach. "*Shall I remove the jacket?*" he thought "B*ut what about the money... she won't see the money if I take out the jacket!*" He couldn't understand why his last minute trick was not working. Worse: she was now showing signs that, despite her timid smile, she would like the interview to be over as soon as possible. Her replies were shorter and she looked at her watch several times.

François tried to stretch the encounter, using all tricks on the book, but he came to realize that he was fighting a lost battle. With nothing more than a brief handshake, she left the room 20 minutes after the meeting had started. Baffled by such a contrast between the girl's reputation and her actual behavior with him, François remained seated in the meeting room, trying to understand the reasons for his failure. He couldn't come up with none, except the fact that maybe there were girls out there that weren't fascinated by his money, power and charisma. "*Exceptions to the rule!*" he thought, when he finally got up from his chair and left the office.

The girl left the company and the manager continued with his occasional affairs with female colleagues. The only novelty was that the organization had suddenly become volatile, with leadership changes that made his job not as secured as before. He also sensed that the lack of prestige in a customer service position was even bigger than expected, and that his reputation was suffering. After a few conversations with his counter-part, where they both shared their disappointment and insecurity, François decided it was time to leave. After a few more months, he asked to be transferred back to his old position. The request was accepted and he left the customer support world for good.

His activities as a womanizer were also left behind. He had not changed, but he was getting a bit too old to play that game. That, or his success rate was far from what he expected. Anyway, back home, his advances with the opposite sex would not be taken as lightly and a false step could eventually mean the end of his career. François, the account manager continued while his other side, as a flamboyant womanizer, retired... at least for a while!

13 - A CHRISTMAS FLOOD

THE CENSORED STORIES

Customer service jobs in call centers are usually the lowest entry level point to many corporations. To attract candidates into those positions, company's frequently use a number of tricks. One of them are fancy job titles like "*business executive*", "*partner associate*" or "*account coordinator*". Another way to allure people to those jobs is to lower the requirements so that almost anyone can apply. Former students, freshly out of the university, are usually a target, since they are keen to have their first experience of the corporate world.

However, to these new employees, after a few weeks on the job, it all becomes clear: they were hired to reply to emails and answer (or make) phone calls to not-so-happy people. And they must do it fast. Soon they also realize that, in most companies, customer service people are seen with disdain and almost as second class employees. Of course, nothing of this is expressed directly to them, even when the patronizing behaviors of colleagues from other departments are hardly disguised.

This doesn't happen only on long established

corporations. In new highly technological companies, that are infused with sophisticated ideas and a revolutionary spirit, the scenario is similar. The customer service department of those start-ups often sells itself in the job market as one that will be different from all the others, with a new approach to the concept of customer support. In the end, the job will be the same, with probably just a better office and some extra perks provided. This was the case of a globally successful e-commerce company, that had a very peculiar approach to the way their call center operated.

As a very fast growing company, every department was struggling to adapt to a permanently changing environment. Customer support was no exception, with just an increased handicap: their director was known for being incompetent. With teams placed in several offices, in three different parts of the world, customer service struggled to prioritize their work and make some sense of their daily tasks. Some people were taking phone calls, others were focusing on the never ending emails backlog and, finally, a third group was firefighting between functions, according to the needs of the day.

The confusion was such that employees didn't know what their schedule and duties were until 10AM. At that time, an email would be sent by one of the supervisors, detailing their daily tasks. Besides that, the only target they had was to handle forty emails per day. Knowing this, and to avoid being on the spotlight of their nosy director, employees would chose the easiest customer emails, so they could quickly meet their daily goal. If they would fail to do it, for any reason, they knew the big boss would demand an explanation on why the productivity had been low. The end result was that people avoided handling complicated cases, since they would take more time to solve. To the customer this meant that, the bigger your problem was, the less priority it would have.

The director herself spent most of her time flying around, visiting the different offices, and practicing the only activity where her merits were recognized: networking. She had an incredible ability to spend hours chatting with people that she would meet, regardless of their function or position.

Team buildings and after-work drinks were also one of her strongest points and her reputation as a "party animal" was indeed well deserved. One other duty that would take a significant part of her time was checking English spelling mistakes in her employee's messages. She would often randomly check the emails sent to customers and would be very harsh to anyone that would fail to meet her high grammatical standards.

On the other hand, one of her biggest shortcomings as a leader was failing to set the example for others. In one occasion, while presenting her department to a large audience of partners and colleagues, a few slides of her own creation were displayed in a gigantic screen. Surprisingly (or maybe not) some of the sentences had spelling mistakes.

Another peculiar feature of the director's leadership was when the company organized events or celebrations for all employees. She would always be present while, at the same time, she would limit the number of her own team members who would be allowed to attend those parties. The customer support team would end up feeling discriminated, watching all the other departments enjoy snacks and drinks.

She was also blissfully unaware of her very low levels of popularity among those that worked for her. She was usually very friendly and bubbly with all her team members, bringing them chocolates and gossip magazines, every time she would visit one of the offices. However, most people disliked her lack of organization skills and that she would not lead by example. On the other hand, most of her team managers were subservient, not questioning the instructions given and always ready to please their boss. That's why, in fact, they had been hired. The director wanted to be sure that her authority would remain unchallenged. In the meantime, the department results were weak and customers were left unsatisfied. But who cared about that, when the overall results of the company were so fantastic?

Very few people (if any) knew exactly how clients were really supported, since there were very few reports about customer service activities. Some numbers were issued regularly, but the results were so random, that it was difficult to reach any conclusion. People wondered why the chief operations officer (the director's boss) was not more strict with her, demanding to know what was really going on. Maybe the fact that they were long-time friends, with their respective families taking holidays together, conditioned his behavior. In any case the director kept telling everyone that customer service was doing "wonderfully well"! She had been given a free hand to manage the department and she used that freedom with no restraint.

One of her favorite uses of the freedom she had, was to make decisions based on a whim. Once she canceled all the vacations of her team members for four consecutive months. She based her decision on the assumption that "they were going to be very busy and they would need all hands on deck!" People were left frustrated to have such a long period without days off and to add insult to injury, most of that time they actually had very little work to do.

Another of her sudden decisions was made during the December holidays season. She gave instructions to her team members that they all had to work on Christmas eve. On one side, it made sense that a business like an e-commerce should have customer support coverage during that day. However, something important was missing: there were no reports that showed how much work they should expect to have on December 24th, so nobody knew how many people were really needed... if any at all. Adding to that, no other department in the company was going to work on that day, reducing dramatically the capability of solving any real issue. Nonetheless, the decision was taken and the majority of team members had to come to terms with the idea of having to work, before they could join their families for Christmas celebrations.

One of the offices of the company was located in an industrial park, isolated from any nearby towns. On that Christmas eve, when the customer service team arrived to the office, they found the park deserted, as most companies were closed for the day. Without a living soul around, even within their own building, they sat down at their desks and got ready for the daily routines. The director had previously communicated that she would be available in case of need, as she was taking the day off to spend it with the family. After one hour, the backlog had been handled and there was no work to do.

The team waited for phone calls to arrive or emails to land on their inbox queue. Nothing was happening, everything was quiet and they started to wonder what they were suppose to be doing there. Hours passed and the only noticeable event was the relentless rain that kept falling outside, making the day even more miserable. With nothing to do, some of the team members decided to play ping pong, using the table in the employees relaxing area. It was an attempt to avoid boredom and get the time to pass quicker. Lunch time came and there was still no work.

After lunch, one of the team members needed to go and get something out of her car. When she opened the main door downstairs she realized that the area was flooded and there was no way how she would be able to get to her car. With the rain continuously falling, the situation could only get worse. When she told this to her colleagues upstairs, one of the more senior team members decided to call the director and explain the urgency of the situation. At the beginning of the call, with the background noise of Christmas carols, the director joyfully wished a "Merry Christmas" to her employee.

She quickly dismissed all concerns from her employee and actually thought that the isssue was not important enough to interrupt her baking duties. She had some wonderful mince pies in the oven and she was just preparing a delicious Christmas pudding. She assured her employee that the flood would recede as the day progressed and told her to remind the team of their professional duties and obligations. The call was quickly over, since the director needed to check on her pies.

Stunned by their boss´s attitude, the team watched as the rain intensified and the flood progressed, now reaching the parking lot where the employees had their cars. They had to do something. One of them decided to call the local office manager and ask for help. Immediately, after being informed, the manager told he would talk with their boss and instructed them to leave the office without delay. Ten minutes later, he called them back to say that the director had finally agreed in letting them go home. Regretfully, it was too late. They were unable to leave the building, as the water level was too high. Emergency services had to be called.

The fire department arrived and managed to evacuate everyone from the office, even allowing some of them to return home using their own vehicles. One of those employees was not so lucky though: while trying to avoid a part of the road that was heavily flooded, the car hit some rubble and the bottom of the vehicle was severely damaged. Unable to proceed, the employee was forced to take a ride home with one of the colleagues. Needless to say the company never took any responsibility for the accident, refusing to pay for the car repair.

These, and other incidents that followed, weakened the reputation of the customer support director. If her blunders with her own department were still tolerated, her inability to cooperate with other teams made her highly unpopular with other managers. She would never keep her promises and would often interfere with issues that were not of her own responsibility. Everybody realized by now that she was good for a chat, but useless to work with. Eventually, the chief operations officer could no longer ignore the lack of results and the complaints he received from many of her colleagues.

He gave her, nonetheless, the opportunity of an honorable discharge and her dismissal was presented to the rest of the company as a decision that she had taken herself. Given the context and her background, very few believed that she had left the job out of her own initiative but, in this case, the important thing was that she was gone. After all, it's an unwritten rule in most corporations that senior leaders always leave with dignity, no matter how incompetent they were for the position.

14 - THE SMARTPHONE GIRL

THE CENSORED STORIES

SRi LENKA " the Tear of Europe"

On this particular company the job of receptionist was a promising one. There were not a lot of requirements needed from a candidate to be able to do the work but at the same time, there were very promising perspectives for those that took the role. Daily duties could hardly be considered hard work: taking some (very few) external phone calls, welcome visitors and guide them to the correct offices or meeting rooms, distribute the post and... chat endlessly in the internal messaging tool.

Lenka was very pleased with how easy the job was. More than anything else, she was happy that it allowed her to keep regular contact with almost all departments in the building and particularly, with their bosses. She was very keen in showing her availability to be helpful, especially to those that would potentially be useful in getting her career moving forward.

She never lost an opportunity to expand her network and she was soon easily recognized as the kind and smiling girl, who was always ready to help and very keen to acquire knowledge outside of her normal tasks. Lenka was also clever enough to "hang out" with the *"right"* crowd and she was regularly seen taking coffee with some of the influential people in the office.

Yes, she had a few hiccups along the way, especially when some of her colleagues noticed that she was often having Skype calls with *"Italian friends"* during working hours. However, her pleasant attitude and swiftness when completing her tasks kept her in the good grace of almost everybody.

Eventually, Lenka's efforts were rewarded. A job opening came up in the HR Shared Services team and she was tipped off as the ideal candidate. After a single interview, she was offered the position and her short lived career as a receptionist came to an end. Among her news responsibilities she now had to manage, control and provide accessibility to the company's mobile phone users.

The job seemed easy enough and as a bonus (even if that was out of her pay grade) she was given the chance to ask for her own mobile phone. The request was immediately approved by her new manager. Soon enough she was enjoying one of the biggest perks you can have when working for a multinational company: the free use of a company smartphone. Lenka was new in the team but she managed to have access to a benefit that many of her colleagues could only dream about. Her dedication to the company was finally paying off.

The corporate rules, however, were very rigorous

concerning the use of mobile devices: they were only supposed to be used for business purposes but, in reality, the vast majority of employees would also use them for private reasons. Another rule was that access to social networks was blocked and monthly bills regularly monitored, meaning that any excessive amount would have to be justified.

Lenka, however, thought that these policies were not applicable to her position. She used her natural sympathy to get in the good graces of the people working with her and, with that, she soon managed to have social networks unblocked on her own device. She was in frequent contact with the phone provider and they never hesitated to follow her instructions. As well as social networks, Lenka also had premium text messages unblocked on her phone. This was very useful as she could travel in the city's public transportation system for *"free"*, since tickets could be bought through a text message service. She was now enjoying free rides, paid by the company.

These small perks couldn't hurt such a big company like the one she worked for – Lenka thought, while surfing through her personal page in a social network (during working hours, naturally). Her good looks and natural charm conquered many admirers among her colleagues but also brought her the unavoidable jealous critics. Nonetheless, she enjoyed her increasing popularity and daydreamed about the career possibilities that were slowly arising in the horizon.

Lenka's success in her professional life was emulated

somehow in her private life. She had a legion of admirers, most of them foreigners, that were competing for her attention and favors. A number of them would shower her with expensive gifts, that she would parade in the office, with obvious pride. Others would go even further and invite her to trips to exotic destinations, where they could both have a relaxed time together.

One of those trips took her (and one of those admirers) to the distant island of Sri Lanka. There she spent two weeks enjoying the delights of tropical beaches, five-star hotels and exquisite gourmet food. Evidently, those glamorous moments had to be shared with friends and fans. Numerous selfies were taken and pictures of beautiful landscapes were constantly filling her posts in social networks. She loved to make everyone aware of her marvelous adventures and achievements. For that purpose, the company's smartphone became very handy indeed, allowing her regular access to the internet for *"free"*.

Back to work, a few weeks later, our heroine was surprised to be summoned to a meeting by her manager. His tone was grave and the expression serious. With a copy of the monthly phone bill in his hand, he requested an explanation for the outrageous amount that the company would have to pay and he, as a manager, was requested to approve. According to his words, there had been an unauthorized use of internet network in Sri Lanka, which was expensive, especially if you were using a foreign sim-card. He demanded a justification.

To the average employee, this would have been a very uncomfortable situation to be in. However, Lenka was far from being the average employee. She knew that her manager had a weak spot for her, as he had already tried to flirt a number of times. Full of self confidence, she openly admitted using roaming for personal use. At the same time, she also candidly confessed that she never thought that the cost of using it would be so high.

The manager was not impressed with the explanation. He pointed angrily to the bill, outlining the number where the Sri Lanka network charges were clearly visible: "*Why were you using your work phone on a private trip?* - he asked - *I know that, once in a while, we all use it for private matters, but this bill is way too high! Weren't you aware of how expensive would be to use the company phone in such a place?*"

Lenka used the most candid expression in her repertoire and replied: "*I thought Sri Lanka was part of the European Union...*"
The manager had indeed a weak spot for her, but the breach of company regulations was so obvious that he could not ignore the facts. The site leadership committee was called to decide the future of Lenka. With all the office leaders gathered in a meeting room, the manager explained that he could not approve such a high amount for a mobile phone bill, much less when it had been used privately. Therefore, he suggested that the only option available was to have the employee dismissed from her job.

Big corporations are managed by very strict rules and

procedures. The senior leadership is also keen in establishing a culture that is supposedly embodied by those who work for the company. These high values need to be shared by all offices, regardless of their location in the world. One of the most important principles, generally considered as universal, is that all employees should be treated equally. However, on Lenka's case, all guidelines, processes, rules and requirements were, mysteriously enough, quickly forgotten.

To the manager's surprise, the committee verdict slowly turned out to be a judgment about him and not about Lenka. The country director, that lead the meeting, appeared to be more interested in questioning his management capabilities than in discussing Lenka's phone bill issue. *"Why did you authorize the use of a company mobile phone by someone that was not entitled to it?"* - the director asked, with an aggressive tone in his voice. *"Why were you approving her monthly phone bills when she should have none at all?"* - he continued - *"Why did you permit such an abusive behavior?"*. The manager tried to answer but he didn't know what to say. He tried to mumble some justification and the gathering soon came to a dead-end. Another meeting was scheduled, when a final decision would be made.

The truth was that all of those questions had a point and the manager knew it: Lenka shouldn't have ever been given the opportunity to have a company phone. That was a clear breach of corporate rules and he had no valid argument to justify why he had authorized it. He felt he had been caught by her charm and, as a result, he made bad decisions. He was now on trial and Lenka's case became a secondary topic.

As scheduled, during the following meeting, justice was delivered: the manager got told off and was instructed to review his leadership methods. Considering all the possibilities that were on the table (including his dismissal), he was quite happy to receive such a "mild punishment". As to what Lenka concerned, she lost access to her mobile phone realizing, at last, that Sri Lanka was not a member of the European Union. The phone bill was paid and the case was closed.

A few months went on and the manager, unable to recover from the effects of the whole episode, resigned and left the company. Lenka, on the other hand, quickly recovered and kept on working like if nothing had happened. A new manager came and her reputation was completely restored, while her popularity continued to increase. In less than a year she was made a Communications Manager and a new mobile phone was given to her, as one of the benefits that came with the new position. A new world of opportunities was again available. Lenka was happier than ever.

15 - TERRIBLE BOSSES

THE CENSORED STORIES

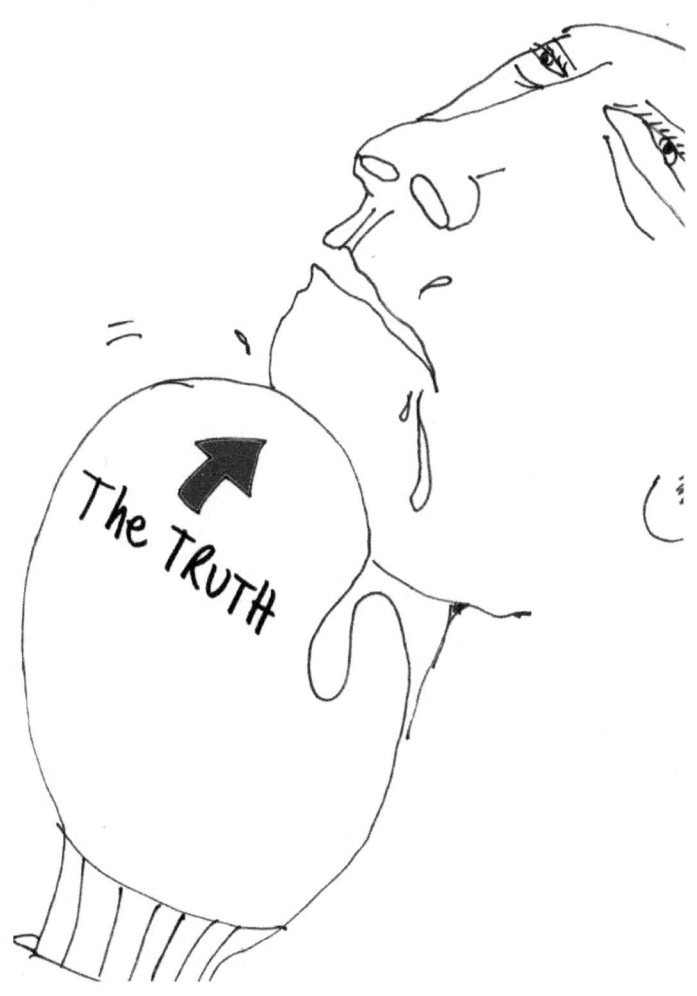

THE CENSORED STORIES

An old-fashioned pub, in one of the city's historical neighborhoods, was the monthly meeting place of three friends. Peter, Joseph and Patrick used to work for the same company in a not-so-distant past. Since then, their careers had followed different paths but their friendship remained. They were all ex-pats that had been living in the country for several years. The three of them married locally and Peter and Joseph had children. One other thing they had in common was the fact that they were all managers, although working for different corporations.

To keep their friendship alive, they got into the habit of meeting every month in the same place. The gathering would usually happen on a Friday evening and they would spend their time talking about life in general and, quite often, about work. That pub was usually crowded but somehow they always managed to get the same table, in a corner where the wall was decorated with old pictures from the city. After the usual friendly handshakes, beers would be ordered and soon everyone started talking.

On this occasion, Patrick was the most talkative of the three, as he had recently joined a new company and had fresh news to share:

"So the other day I was going to have a meeting with my boss and, when we were about to start, she told me "One of your team members is in a meeting room with someone from a different department. Go and check what is it about."

"Why would she ask you to do that?" inquired Joseph, while sipping his beer.

"Well, from what I understand, she is a kind of a control freak. She saw them in a meeting room and instead of asking herself what they were doing there, she told me to do it. So there I went, apologized for interrupting and asked what the meeting was about. It was just a job interview for a different department. That was fine by me so I returned to the meeting with my boss and gave her that explanation."

"Was she happy about it?" asked Peter

"No", replied Patrick with a smile, *"She said team members shouldn't be having job interviews during their shifts. So I reckon she meant that, in order to be interviewed for other jobs in the company, those meetings have to take place after normal working hours! I can already imagine the scene. One of my guys comes to me and says "Hey boss, will you approve one hour of overtime for me today? I have a job interview, you know!"*

Everybody at the table laughed. Patrick continued:

"But if you think that's ridiculous, the other day she complained that one of my team members arrived late to the 8AM shift. Again, I was told to go and check what happened. So I went to his manager and asked for the daily schedule. The explanation was simple: that guy's shift began at 9AM, but he had decided to come a bit early, since there was a lot of work to do. Basically, he was being finger pointed for his dedication to the company.

"And what did your boss say?" asked Peter, *"Doesn't she check things before giving instructions? I hope she at least apologized."*

"Well, she has over 200 people in her department so I'm sure she has more important things to do than checking on people's attendance. When I told her that the employee had actually arrived earlier to work, she made a confused expression and answered that this was not good either. I couldn't get her to explain why it was not right to come early to work so... I guess she is unable to recognize a mistake or to admit she was wrong!"

At this moment Joseph and Peter were looking at Patrick with concerned expressions. Their friend looked tired and worn out.

"That's not going to work for you, is it Patrick?" said Joseph.

"We will see." he replied, with a discouraged expression in his face. *"It's still early days but I can't say that I have reasons to be optimistic. My boss seems to be the kind of person that likes to be popular among employees but, behind their*

back, is telling her own managers to be nasty to them. I hope I will be able to deal with that or I won't stay long in this company."

By now, the tone of the conversation was far from being joyful, so Joseph decided to lighten up things:

"Well, Patrick, at least you don't have to carry your boss back to the hotel room. Two weeks ago, I went on a business trip with one of my directors. After the usual meetings we went for after-work drinks with some of our local colleagues. He got so drunk that he could barely stand. To make matters worse, he weights more than 150 kilos, so imagine how difficult it was for me to carry him from the taxi upstairs to his hotel room. I thought I would have to help him put on his pajama but, luckily, he was able to stumble to his bed, where he immediately fell asleep. Yikes! The next day, he begged me not to tell anyone about the incident."

Everyone at the table was laughing. Peter ordered another round of beers and carried on:

"I never had the "luck" to carry a heavy boss on my back" said he, in a sarcastic tone, *"but speaking about hotel rooms, reminds me of a boss I had. He was the country manager of this huge company but he didn't allow any of the employees to chose a hotel for visitors."*

"What do you mean?", asked Patrick. *"He made the hotel reservations himself?"*

"No, we would take care of that but only after he had chosen the hotel first. You see, once I had colleagues from another office visiting us and they asked if they could stay in a different place

than last time. So I took the liberty of making a reservation for them in a cheaper hotel. One hour later, I was getting a call from the country manager, asking me why I had not "followed the process". I replied that our guests didn't like the usual place so I had booked them in a different one, that was actually cheaper to the company. He ordered me to change the bookings back to the original hotel and told me not to try that "stunt" again. He sounded really pissed off!"

"I guess that even in big companies some people cannot resist the temptation of making money on the side" Joseph commented. *"Probably he had a "parallel contract" with the hotel and received a "commission" for every guest he sent there. I once knew a manager that did something similar, but in a different field: she hired the same DJ for all of the company's events. When people complained that they were tired of listening the same music, she said she couldn't get anyone else to do the job. Soon, employees found out that the DJ was, actually, her boyfriend, so by hiring him she was assuring a supplement to the "family" income!*

"Well, my current boss is looking for a different kind of bonus". Peter continued, *"His problem is to keep his pants up. He just got married and, on the first meeting we had after his return from honeymoon, he made a raunchy remark about one of my team members."*

"Freshly out of his honeymoon, eh?" said Patrick with a smile.

"Yes, indeed" replied Peter, *"We were about to start the meeting and he saw her passing by. As soon as the meeting room door closed, he said: "I would definitely take that one with me on a business trip!" When he saw the shocked faces of the*

other people in the room, he apologized saying it had been a "bad joke".

"Maybe he just lacks sense of humor" added Joseph, hardly disguising the irony in his voice.

"Maybe" continued Peter, *"Although he recently hired a very pleasantly looking lady for a position reporting directly to him. This, despite having other internal candidates with a lot more experience and a good performance record. I imagine that the lady must have tremendous job interviewing skills or has qualifications that are unknown to her colleagues. Anyway, I'm sure a director like him is perfectly objective in his choices, right? Otherwise, why would he have that job?*

Once again all the three friends burst into laughter. Patrick continued the conversation, in a playful mood:

"If you think that's funny, let me tell you what happened when my boss gave me the mid-year review for my performance. After 20 minutes of compliments and telling me how my experience was important to the company, she asks: "Why did you accept a lower salary when you joined us?"

"Wait a minute" interrupted Joseph, *"She was asking you why you had a lower salary than the others in the team? Wasn't she the one hiring you?"*

"No, another director did it. Anyway" carried on Patrick, *"I told her I didn't know that my salary was that low. After all, it's company policy that we shouldn't discuss openly each others salaries. Still, I added that I was happy she had reached that conclusion and hopefully it would be fixed soon."*

"So you got a pay rise, right?" asked Peter with enthusiasm.

"Nope!" replied Patrick

"How come?" questioned Joseph with a surprised look in his eyes. *"She told you were good and that you were not paid enough so... why didn't she do something about it?"*

"I don't know. I don't understand why she brought the topic of my "poor salary" if she didn't intend to do something about it. She decided that I should "prove myself once again during the next 6 months..." This way she keeps me on the cheap side while now I have the imaginary carrot of a salary pay rise in the future to keep me going. Strange logic, it's all I can say."

Patrick still smiled, but it was a forced smile on his face. His two table companions had expressions of disbelief and resignation. They were quiet for a while and beer glasses got empty. Peter broke the silence between them:

"I sometimes wonder if we are just unlucky or if normal bosses are that difficult to come by nowadays. I have had some good ones in the past but I don't even ask for that any more. Just a normal boss would be enough."

"You mean someone that is capable of doing his job, has sufficient past experience, is concerned about his team and tries to be as fair as possible with his employees?" asked Joseph, again sounding sarcastic.

"Is that asking for too much?" replied Peter.

"No", answered Joseph, "but I guess that then you are missing the most important qualities.

"And those are...?"

"That a good boss should always put the company ahead of the welfare of his team and be willing to sacrifice his personal life. That he is required to present results no matter how. Most of all that he should be popular among his superiors and feared by his employees. This is the profile that fits better with what companies are looking for in managers nowadays. If you have that, you can pretty much forget about all the rest."

"Then it seems that we are doomed!" answered Peter, finishing his glass of beer. The others nodded in agreement.

"I guess you are right, my friend", replied Joseph, requesting the bill from the waiter. *"In the meantime, let's enjoy it while we can and go home to what really is important: our families."*

THE CENSORED STORIES

TO BE CONTINUED...

If you would like to share some of your unique corporate stories with me, please feel free to do so, using the contacts below:

Email: hangingman@mail.com

Facebook: HangingManThe

Instagram: hangingmanThe

Twitter: HangingmanThe

www.ingramcontent.com/pod-product-compliance
Lightning Source LLC
Chambersburg PA
CBHW071424180526
45170CB00001B/209